Deliver Us From Evil

Learning From the Past

Deryl S. Lampkin

How To Gain Victory Over Evil & Refresh Your Relationships

Copyright © 2014 Deryl S. Lampkin
All rights reserved.

This book is protected by the copyright laws of the United States of America. This book may not be copied or reprinted for commercial gain or profit. The use of short quotations or occasional page copying for personal or group study is permitted and encouraged. Permission will be granted for larger use of the text upon request.

This book and eBook is licensed for your personal enjoyment only. This book may not be re-sold or given away to other people. If you would like to share this book with another person, please purchase an additional copy for each reader. If you're reading this book and did not purchase it, or it was not purchased for your use only, then please return to your favorite retailer and purchase your own copy. Thank you for respecting the hard work of this author.

Scripture quotations are from the King James Version of the Bible unless otherwise identified.

ISBN EBook 978-1-942325-00-0
ISBN Paperback 978-1-942325-01-7
ISBN Audio Book 978-1-942325-02-4

Website: www.deryllampkin.com

ACKNOWLEDGEMENTS

I preeminently recognize God, my Heavenly Father, and his awesome and mighty Son, Jesus Christ as the Master of my life and the entire universe. He delivered me from the powers of evil and resurrected me unto newness of life.

This book is dedicated to Robert and Joyce Lampkin, my departed earthly father and mother. I thank God for my father. He imparted much wisdom, knowledge, and skills into my life. My mother introduced me to my Lord and Savior, Jesus Christ, and was instrumental in bringing most of her children to Christ.

This book is also dedicated to Emmanuel Devon Lampkin, my deceased son, whom I love and miss dearly and to Torry, Donisheya, and Richard. May God bless them to read this book and be profoundly influenced by its words.

Finally, and with honor, I acknowledge my pastors, (Dr. Andre and Dr. Kim Sanders) of Kingdom Faith Global Ministries (www.kfgm.org), Dr. Myles Munroe (my spiritual great granddaddy), Mother Rose Marie Bonamy, (my number one fan), Cathy Ferguson (for her extra pair of eyes and listening ears) and my entire Kingdom Faith Global Ministries family. I love you all dearly.

WARNING: THIS BOOK CONTAINS HIGHLY EXPLOSIVE INFORMATION AND REVELATIONS. IF YOU READ AND INTEGRATE THESE PRINCIPLES INTO YOUR WAY OF THINKING, YOU MAY ACTIVATE A TIME-RELEASED SPIRITUAL-LOGICAL EXPLOSION IN YOUR HEART THAT WILL FATALLY DAMAGE AND DESTROY A GREAT DEAL OF THE EVIL AND RELIGIOUS VIEWPOINTS YOU HAVE BEEN HARBORING FOR TOO LONG. PLEASE PROCEED WITH CAUTION. THE LIFE YOU CHANGE JUST MIGHT BE YOUR OWN.

Book Description:

At the root of hurting relationships are misinformation, misunderstandings, and mistrust. *Deliver Us From Evil* reveals life-changing principles to repair your relationships with your spouse, God, and others. The lust of honey, and the love of money, has destroyed countless relationships because, men want to get laid, and women want to get paid. These powerful truths can refresh your relationships and bring you joy. This book is a must-have guide to help you conquer evil.

Throughout history, the greatest men and women down to the least have fallen prey to lust. *Deliver Us From Evil* re-examines powerful insights from the past that reveal, why even those who appear to be the godliest, sometimes fail morally. Learn the secrets to consistently defeating sin and evil influences in your life.

We must become better equipped to combat the evil forces that bombards our lives today and continually seeks to corrupt and destroy our moral and spiritual fiber. The same tactics and strategies that Satan used on Adam and Eve, is still being used on us today.

From the beginning of creation and throughout history, some of the greatest men have fallen prey to one of the most powerful tactics and strategies of the devil. In this book, you will learn what causes great men to fall and forfeit their power, influence, and good reputation. You will also learn other eye-opening insights that will be beneficial on your journey in the Lord.

A journey back in time will reveal Satan's simple, yet powerful, maneuvers he uses to spread his evil works throughout the earth. This book exposes his crafty devices and will empower believers to have more successful and drama-free lives.

Adam and Eve made certain critical mistakes that continue to influence our lives today. We can be delivered from evil and experience true victory if we learn the secrets of Satan's strategies that he used on them.

What Writing This Book Has Taught Me
In writing this book, I have come to understand, respect, and appreciate more profoundly, the awesomeness and value of a woman. I have also come to understand that if a man does not carefully choose his wife, that careless choice will end up costing him in many ways. The same is also true for a woman.

God has endowed a woman with extraordinary influential power. Although she was made to be the weaker vessel in terms of physical strength, she has the power to influence men and influence their world in ways that no other species can. She has the power to build a man up and cause him to rise to great prominence.

Conversely, she can invade the life of a prominent man and single-handedly strip him of all that he has worked hard and long to accomplish. The positive use of her power can bring her great honor and glory, yet the negative use of her power can severely demean her and bring her great shame and disgrace.

Both men and women are subject to being influenced by evil forces. Our carnal nature causes us to be susceptible to sin. Therefore, in order for us to be delivered from evil, we need the power of the Holy Spirit and the influence and guidance of the Word of God to successfully lead us away from temptation and to deliver us from all evil.

Disclaimer: As you read this book, you will find places where hypothetical dialogues and conversations were intentionally inserted to add a little humor and expand your imagination. These are **INTENDED FOR ENTERTAINMENT PURPOSES ONLY**. Do not take these conjectures to be either factual or scriptural.

Some thoughts expressed in this book are intended to be generalities, and so they may not apply to your own specific situation. If you encounter any of these thoughts, do not trip out. Just accept that you are the exception to the rule.

Target Audience: The primary audience of this book is Christian believers and truth seekers. I wrote this book to share with them insightful revelations and principles that will enable them to defeat sin and prevent evil from reigning in their lives.

Nevertheless, the intended readership is not limited to Christian believers only. The content also deals with issues that affect all people, regardless of their social, economic, religious, racial, ethnic, political, or cultural preferences or statuses. Therefore, this book is for everyone because everyone encounters and deals with some form of sin and evil.

For those who are mature in the Word and already know, understand, and practice the principles underscored in this book, you may find additional illumination about things you may not have been aware of fully. For those who have not been so enlightened, I promise you will find many eye opening nuggets of truth and revelation to savor and remember. Enjoy!

Table of Contents

ACKNOWLEDGEMENTS i
PREFACE 1
INTRODUCTION 6
CHAPTER ONE The Broad-Spectrum Purpose of Life 11
CHAPTER TWO Pre-Creation And The Creation of the World 18
CHAPTER THREE The Creation of Man 35
CHAPTER FOUR Peace on Earth In The Garden of Eden 44
CHAPTER FIVE The Birth of Evil Misinformation Causes You To Miss Out 51
CHAPTER SIX Woman: The Most Powerful Creature on Earth 73
CHAPTER SEVEN A Walk On The Wild Side:
Evil Gets Progressively Worse As It Advances 90
CHAPTER EIGHT It's All in the Mind 99
CHAPTER NINE The Curse of Evil 113
CHAPTER TEN Living Holy Before God
and Restoring the Garden 126
Important Take-Aways and Things To Remember 135
About The Author 144

PREFACE

When I began writing this book, I originally entitled it *"In the Beginning"*. As I endeavored further and delved deeper into the work, I sensed it taking a sharp turn toward Adam and Eve. The book was clearly turning toward relationships and how the advent of evil had entered a peaceful and harmonious environment and brought sin, shame, and discord to the first love relationships.

The original love relationship was between God and Adam, and it was a great relationship. However, at that time, there was no other compatible species on earth like Adam. Therefore, God made him a helpmate called woman and gave her the name, Eve. This relationship between Adam and Eve was the first love relationship between two humans of opposite sexes. It was then I realized that a change in the book's title was in order.

The Bible story started out with the Creation, however, once the first couple arrived on the scene, all the good that God had created was about to change. Once sin entered the world through Eve and then Adam, life on earth was never going to be the same.

The evil one called Satan or the devil and the serpent entered the garden to alter this picture perfect existence. He entered the world of humans with an evil agenda. He wanted to destroy the harmonious relationship between God, Adam, and Eve. Satan approached the woman because he understood the power she possessed to influence the man. Satan recognized that he could strategically use the woman to dethrone the man and thus cause enmity between God and humanity.

We have been contending with evil forces that seek to keep us at odds with God since the fall of humanity. As long as we are at odds with God, ignorant of whom we are, and oblivious to the real power we possess, we will continuously live defeated substandard lives and be conquered by evil forces. Satan will continue to render us powerless to overcoming evil and living holy before God as long as we remain ignorant of the Truth and are disobedient.

For this reason, I have written this book that I may share with you valuable information and revelations that will empower you to be delivered from evil, reestablish a continuous harmonious relationship with God, your mate, and others and live a victorious and fulfilled life before God, well removed from Satan and his annoying evil.

Everyone Is At Risk of Contracting Evil

In this world, we all deal with the struggles, adversities, and hassles of life. We refer to these as the evils of the world. In general, we consider evil to be *anything that causes others or ourselves hurt, harm, pain, suffering, or misfortune.* Most people sincerely want to avoid the evils of life, but unfortunately, evil is like the energizer bunny, it keeps on going.

Evil is present and at work virtually in one form or another everywhere we turn. It has infiltrated our personal lives, our homes, our children, our marriages, our communities, our businesses, our churches, our schools, and our governments. There is no area of life that is off limits to evil.

No one is exempt from experiencing some expression of evil. Your race, color, nationality, economic status, education, or religion does not matter. Everyone is at risk of contracting sin and evil. Some of the evils we experience are of course due to our own making. Other people intentionally cause some, and sometimes evil happens to us unintentionally or accidentally.

We constantly struggle with all kinds of issues and problems in life. We struggle with our finances, our health, family matters, business, work, car problems, children problems, marital problems — the list goes on and on. Life did not start out this way. In the beginning, there were no problems. When we first come into this world, our problems are minuscule or nonexistent. Then as we grow and develop, we find that our problems and issues grow as well.

Many of these problems and issues we manufacture ourselves. In other words, we are the creators of some of our problems. They come about because of things we do or fail to do, things we say or do not say, things we think or do not think about, and things we think we know and things we do not know. Sometimes others cause our problems. However, many times we allow those others to bring their problems into our own lives. In most cases, however, we do play a critical role in creating and manufacturing our own evils.

Of course, we can blame it all on the devil or others and make it seem as though someone else is to blame. That excuse in and of itself is a problem. When we think in that way, we are not taking personal responsibility. The devil may in fact have suggested a bad idea to us, but we are still the one who accepted and acted on that bad idea. The devil has no power to make us do anything. He only suggests things, creates situations, and present challenges. We make the ultimate decision to do or not do what the devil wants.

God could have easily sent Satan straight to Hell; instead, He cast him down to earth. Satan is the tempter and tester of humanity. God uses him to reveal the content of our character and determine if we are wise or susceptible to evil. If we are truly made of godly characteristics, it will be evident by our test results. If we lack godly character, that will be evident also when we are tested.

Therefore, the devil is not the real problem. The problem lies in whether we have or do not have godly character. If we have it, we will defeat the devil and be victorious in every area of our lives. If we do not have a godly character, we will suffer defeat.

We Have the Ministry of Reconciliation

God expects us to proactively conquer life by understanding what He intended, and then doing whatever is necessary to bring our life into conformity to the Will of God. He has equipped believers with His power (the Holy Spirit) and has made His Word available to us.

In the world, there will always be problems until God exterminates the earth and purges it of all that offends Him. In the meantime, we should diligently do our part to change the world for the better. After all, we are the ones who are living on earth, and we have to contend with all the evil we allow to come into our world.

God has given believers the power to overcome all things. He has given us the ministry of reconciliation. It is our task and responsibility to bring everything that is out of alignment with God back into alignment with God. We must not see the evils of the world as mere problems, but instead as challenges and opportunities, that we can use to glorify God by using His power within us to change ungodly situations and disorders, from evil to good, and from darkness to light.

The work of the ministry is about positively affecting the world with God's Love and the influence of His Kingdom. When Jesus was on earth, he was continuously confronting the evils of the world and exercising power over them. He made people who were sick and diseased well again. When he encountered people possessed of devils, he cast out their demons. He set people free who were in bondage to sin. He clearly demonstrated that the Kingdom of God was present and able to affect every facet of life.

Most of us have not grown to that level of exercising the power of God as Jesus and Paul did; however, exercising love and preventing evil from using our bodies and minds as a military base and a manufacturing and distribution facility for evil is still well within our reach. It is a matter of making up our minds to obey God and do what He commands. It is not rocket science.

God Has a Purpose for the Devil
When God kicked the devil out of Heaven, He could have easily destroyed him. Instead, He cast him down to earth for a purpose. The devil is here to challenge us and to prove us worthy. Do you remember how God purposely pointed Job out to Satan and gave the devil permission to test Job? Remember, how the Holy Spirit deliberately led Jesus into the wilderness for the expressed purpose of being tested by the devil. God intentionally allows the devil to roam the earth, so the devil can prove and clearly distinguish who is of God and who is not.

The Devil Is Not All Bad
Yes, the devil is evil, harmful, and an enemy of God and man. However, the devil is not all bad. God uses the devil in strategic ways to benefit both man and God. If there were no devil or evil in the world, there would be no motivation for man to seek God. If we could do anything we wanted to do without any consequences or ill effects, then there would be no need for laws, rules, and regulations.

We would never see a real need for God if our actions did not produce undesirable effects in our lives. Good would not stand out if we did not have a negative opposite to compare good to clearly. The effects of sin and evil are what bring many of us to the realization that we need God. Darkness is what makes us appreciate light. Darkness conceals everything from us, but light reveals everything to us.

God uses the devil to test and develop us. Tests reveal what we know and understand and what we do not know and understand. Tests also reveal our strengths and weaknesses. Our weaknesses reveal what we need to pray for and where we need God's help.

Many people go to church, quote the Scriptures, and talk the talk. Nevertheless, the people who will dwell with God forever are those that talk the talk and also walk the walk. They are the ones who live their lives in alignment with the Word and the Spirit of God and cease to live according to the ways of the world and the lusts of the flesh, and thus prove by their resistance to the devil and their righteous living that they truly belong to God.

Where to Find the Answers to Overcoming Evil

There are answers and solutions for overcoming the struggle of evil. These answers cannot be found in the world, because the world is part of the problem. These answers cannot even be found in religions and many of the churches of the world, because these too have become part of the problem.

The answers are found in the Word of Truth. The record of sin entering the world is found in the Bible in *Genesis* in the third chapter. In my own studies, I have found that by going back to the beginning and reexamining how sin and evil entered the world, we can more vividly see and understand how to be delivered from evil and how to help others also be set free.

The Power to Rise Above Evil

The goal of this book is to share some of the insightful principles and revelations I have discovered while exploring the first three chapters of *Genesis*, which have liberated my thinking and enabling me to be truly delivered from evil. We can rise above evil and overcome it rather than letting it exercise its control over us.

Jesus has delivered us from the power of sin from a spiritual and legal perspective. However, experientially we still battle with sin, and evil continues to plague our lives and the world. We must rise to a level of maturity that enables us to be steadfast and immovable in the mist of evil forces coming against us. At a matured level, evil has no power or effect on us internally, although evil may externally come against us as it did with Jesus, Paul, Job, and many other believers. It is like when God sent plagues on the Egyptians, but the plagues had no effect on the children of Israel.

INTRODUCTION

What Is Evil?
Evil is a manifestation of diabolical influences and activity. Evil is *anything that produces hurt, harm, or damage, with a malicious intent.* It can be segmented into three major groups. These three groups are common or normal evils, abnormal evils, and extreme evils. Common evils are the evils that virtually all humans are subjected to in life, such as lust, lying, cheating, envy, hatred, drama, disobedience, and rebellion.

Abnormal evils are those evils typically perpetrated by avid lawbreakers. These evils include murder, terrorism, treason, drug addiction, sexual perversions, robbery, and drug dealing. These secondary evils are not acts that the majority of people commit. Only a select minority engages in them.

Extreme evils are the evils that come from the abyss and from the extreme dark side of evil. They are very freaky, monstrous, unexplainable, raw, uncut, evils. They are evils like witchcraft, devil worship, demon possession, voodoo, sorcery, and divination. Most of us never see this kind of evil close up and personally, except on TV and in the movies.

This book deals primarily with the level one or common evil. Common evil is universal to all humans because of the sinful human nature that we inherited from Adam. Common evil is the evil that naturally flows from our carnal nature. Abnormal evil is the result of individuals who willfully choose to break the laws of God and man and go beyond common evil. Extreme evil is the active engagement of human and diabolical forces that are uniting to wage war against God and humanity. Since most of us do not personally wrestle with level two and three evils, this book will only focus on level one evil.

We Long to Be Free of Evil
Back in the beginning when God first created and bought forth the heavens and the earth, after he completed his work of creation, He

declared it very good. However, before Adam and Eve had their first child, something went terribly wrong. Sin entered the world, and ever since that moment, humans have been contending with the forces of evil.

We long to live in a world of love, peace, joy, prosperity, and a world where there is no pain, suffering, or presence of evil. Nonetheless, evil seems to plague our world continuously and progressively. In spite of the fact that Jesus came and died for our sins and defeated the devil, sin and evil still runs rampant in our society and we do not seem to be able to eliminate it from our lives. Some people go to church, read the Bible, and pray to God, but evil still seems to increase rather than decrease.

Why is this diabolical force still plaguing us? Why can't we once and for all defeat evil and be rid of it forever? Can we be fully delivered from evil, or is it an incurable spiritual disease that will be with us until death do us part?

The Ball Is in Our Court

The prayer model that Jesus gave to his disciples says, *"Lead us not into temptation but deliver us from evil". (Mathew 6:13)* This is one of several things that Jesus instructed us to pray for. What is beginning to become increasingly evident to me is that it appears that believers are waiting for God to come deal with the sin and evil issues in the world. I am now clearly realizing that God is waiting for us, to rise up and conquer evil.

Jesus came and dealt with evil in the spiritual realm and from a legal perspective. The Holy Spirit is the same exact power that enabled Jesus to defeat sin and evil in the heavenly realm, and it is the same exact power Jesus gave to all who believe in him to use to defeat sin and evil in the earthly realm. It is now our turn and indeed our responsibility to deal with evil in the physical earthly realm and in our personal lives.

We Have the Keys to Bind and Loose

God has given us the keys to His Kingdom. With these keys, we have full access to every aspect of His Kingdom. The keys are the secret principles of the Kingdom of God, and they enable us to permit and forbid things on earth. God has authorized us to bind and put a halt to things that should not be happening on earth and release and unleash things that should be happening on earth. This is why it is written: *Whatsoever we bind on earth will be bound in heaven and whatsoever we loose on earth will be loosed in heaven. (Mathew 16:19), (Mathew 18:18)*

The problem God's saints are experiencing in this area is that we do not know which key opens which door. You can have a very powerful computer loaded with the most powerful software on the planet, but if you do not know how to use what you have, you remain powerless to benefit from all that power you have at your disposal. So likewise, if you have the power of God within you and do not know how to use it, you will remain powerless. Conversely, if you use that power destructively or irresponsibly, you will eventually bring destruction upon yourself and others.

Too many pastors have trained us to be disciples of religion and disciples of them, rather than Disciples of Christ. Saints have been taught the rudiments and rituals of religion rather than the principles and precepts of the Kingdom of God. Consequently, saints are ignorant of how to effectively use the power of the Word and the power of the Holy Spirit to accomplish the Will of God. Although Jesus had much to say about the Kingdom of God, and it was his central theme, most churches and believers know very little about what Jesus actually came to establish.

The very reason we are seeing sin and evil still running rampant on earth is because we are allowing it to run rampant. We are not using the power delivered to us by Jesus to put a stop to it. God has left us in charge of finishing the work of God's business, which is to establish His Kingdom on earth.

It is our job and indeed our responsibility to cleanse the earth of its evils. This cleansing is accomplished by going out into all the world and preaching the gospel and teaching the principles of the Kingdom of God to all peoples, nations, and tongues and not in words only, but by doing good deeds to demonstrate the awesome power of God's Word and Spirit to transform lives. It is not necessary for each of us to launch global ministries to accomplish this task. What God expects us to do is bring the influence of His Kingdom to our personal domains, namely, our homes, neighborhoods, churches, and workplaces.

We Are the Door Entrance to the Earthly Realm
Jesus is the door that allows people to enter the Kingdom of God, but we are the door entrance to the earthly realm. Jesus himself entered the world through a human. Every human being enters the earth through a human woman, including Jesus. Sin and evil enters the world through

people and through people, sin continues to grow and flourish. The Kingdom of God and its righteousness also enters the world through people, and through people, it grows and flourishes throughout the world.

"And God said unto Noah, The end of all flesh is come before me; for the earth is filled with violence through them; and, behold, I will destroy them with the earth." (Genesis 6:13 KJV) Notice that it said, *"The earth is filled with violence through them".*

The problem is that there are more people permitting sin and evil to increase in their mind and body than there are people who are allowing the Spirit of God to use their mind and body to establish the Kingdom of God on earth and permanently eliminate all evil from the earth. We want to be delivered from evil, but we keep perpetuating evil by continuing to think, speak, and do evil. How can we possibly be delivered from evil when we are the very ones who keep delivering more evil into the world?

The Good News Is ... We Are Free at Last!

John the Baptist and Jesus came on the scene to command all people to repent. What they were saying was to stop doing evil and start doing good because the Kingdom of God is well within your reach. Jesus was indicating that the King of the Kingdom of God had arrived to deliver humanity from the power of sin, death, and evil. The Son of God had arrived with the keys and power to defeat evil and has made that power accessible to all those who believe in him and follow his instructions and teachings.

The message of this Kingdom was that, we no longer have to be prisoners of sin and work like slaves to produce evil. We are now free from the power of sin and free to serve God in spirit and in truth. We now have unfettered access to the resources of God. We can now access God directly and ask for whatever we need to accomplish His Will on earth. That is the Good News!

Mathew 3:1 In those days came John the Baptist, preaching in the wilderness of Judaea,

Mathew 3:2 And saying, Repent ye: for the kingdom of heaven is at hand.

Mark 1:14 Now after that John was put in prison, Jesus came into Galilee, preaching the gospel of the kingdom of God,

Mark 1:15 And saying, The time is fulfilled, and the kingdom of God is at hand: repent ye, and believe the gospel.

Romans 6:14 (NLT) Sin is no longer your master, for you no longer live under the requirements of the law. Instead, you live under the freedom of God's grace.

Romans 6:18 (NLT) Now you are free from your slavery to sin, and you have become slaves to righteous living.

Romans 6:19 (NLT) Because of the weakness of your human nature, I am using the illustration of slavery to help you understand all this. Previously, you let yourselves be slaves to impurity and lawlessness, which led ever deeper into sin. Now you must give yourselves to be slaves to righteous living so that you will become holy.

Romans 6:20 (NLT) When you were slaves to sin, you were free from the obligation to do right.

Romans 6:21 (NLT) And what was the result? You are now ashamed of the things you used to do, things that end in eternal doom.

Romans 6:22 (NLT) But now you are free from the power of sin and have become slaves of God. Now you do those things that lead to holiness and result in eternal life.

Hebrews 4:16 Let us therefore come boldly unto the throne of grace, that we may obtain mercy, and find grace to help in time of need.

PRAISE GOD! AND THANK YOU JESUS, FOR BRINGING US SALVATION!

CHAPTER ONE
The Broad-Spectrum Purpose of Life

Man Was Put In Charge Of the Earth

The critical mistakes that Adam and Eve made in the beginning are still affecting our lives today. We forfeited the things that God gave and entrusted to us by disobeying his commandments. The same tricks and strategies Satan used on Adam and Eve are the ones he uses on us today. He is recycling and using updated remixes of his old tricks. There is much we can learn by rediscovering what happened in the beginning. We do not have to keep making the same costly mistakes that others before us made.

In the beginning, God made man first, and afterwards, He fashioned a woman from that man. God made the woman to benefit the man and not the man for the benefit of the woman. She was made to be man's helper and companion. God gave Adam the responsibility of governing the earth, and then saw that he needed help to accomplish that mandate. Eve was God's way of giving Adam a means to procreate and multiply his seed. He also endowed the woman with special abilities that were useful in aiding man to fulfill what God commissioned man to do.

Men have the primary responsibility of maintaining law and order on earth, and God holds man directly responsible for doing so. God is the supreme ruler. Jesus is subordinate to God, man is subordinate to Jesus, the woman is subordinate to man, and children are subordinate to their parents.

1 Corinthians 11:3 But I would have you know, that the head of every man is Christ; and the head of the woman is the man; and the head of Christ is God.

1 Corinthians 11:8 (NLT) For the first man didn't come from woman, but the first woman came from man.

1 Corinthians 11:9 (NLT) And man was not made for woman, but woman was made for man.

Romans 13:1 Let every soul be subject unto the higher powers. For there is no power but of God: the powers that be are ordained of God.

Romans 13:2 Whosoever therefore resisteth the power, resisteth the ordinance of God: and they that resist shall receive to themselves damnation.

Men must come to understand how the devil uses the power of deception and the power of seduction to weaken and strip them of their God-given power and authority. God created man in His image and in His likeness, and once man understands what the image and likeness of God is, he will better see how to be transformed back to that image and regain the power and authority originally granted to man and be restored to his rightful place in the Kingdom of God.

We Have the Wrong Understanding of Life

Many people go through life having little or no understanding of what the purpose of life is, or what the purpose of their life on earth is. For many, life is viewed as a rat race, merely a struggle to survive, and a challenge to succeed in life before they go to the grave. Some see life as a process of getting an education, getting a good job, getting married, buying a house, having children, creating memories, buying stuff, retiring, and then dying.

The purpose and intent of life has been lost, distorted, and perverted over time. In this book, I want to take us back to the beginning. By going back to the foundation, I hope to uncover what was lost and understand what we must do to restore it. What went wrong in the beginning is the same thing that is continuing to go wrong now. From this perspective, there is nothing new under the sun. We are still dealing with the same devil and the same mess, but in a twenty-first century dress.

A Word of Wisdom from a Great Wise Man

King Solomon was said to be the wisest man to ever live. King Solomon was made ruler over the nation Israel, a nation too numerous to count. Solomon realized that his position as king was an overwhelming responsibility. Therefore, he asked God for an understanding and discerning heart, so he would be able to judge God's people rightly.

God was pleased with what Solomon requested of him and God said unto him, "Because you have asked this thing, and have not asked for yourself long life; nei-

ther have asked riches for yourself, nor have asked the life of your enemies; but have asked for yourself understanding to discern judgment; Behold, I have done according to your words: lo, I have given you a wise and an understanding heart; so that there was none like you before you, neither after you shall any arise like unto you. And I have also given you that which you have not asked, both riches, and honor: so that there shall not be any among the kings like unto you all your days." (1 Kings 3:11 - 3:13)

King Solomon, in his day, had the privilege of experiencing virtually everything his heart desired. He was ultra rich, had a thousand drop-dead gorgeous women, and had unparalleled power, knowledge, and wisdom. After experiencing everything life had to offer, he offered us a bit of his wisdom when he said, *"Let us hear the conclusion of the whole matter: Fear God, and keep his commandments: for this is the whole duty of man." (Ecclesiastes 12:13)*

In the *Book of Ecclesiastes*, Solomon repetitiously said that all that life has to offer was *"vanity and vexation of spirit"*. In essence, he was saying that it is worthless and frustrating to chase after the worldly and material things of life because in the end, acquiring stuff is not what really matters most in life. He informed us that based on his extensive knowledge and experience, the only thing that really matters in life and has lasting value is to be in awe of God and do whatever He commands. Everything else is futility and only stresses the mind.

Solomon also had something to say concerning how we come into the world and how we leave it. He said, *"As a man came forth of his mother's womb, naked shall he return to go as he came, and shall take nothing of his labor, which he may carry away in his hand". (Ecclesiastes 5:15)*

Solomon realized that in spite of all the great things he accomplished, he was going to leave the world with the exact same material things he came into the world with, which was nothing. Perhaps, because we do not know the real purpose of life, we tend to spend life trying to acquire things that we will ultimately leave behind anyway when we depart.

Vast numbers of people spend their time on earth trying to survive, get rich, and chase their vanity. In the final analysis, many lose both their souls and everything they spent their lives pursuing. What does it profit a person if they gain great wealth and accomplish great achievements at the expense of their soul? Can all their wealth redeem their soul from Hell? Your eternal soul has far more value than your temporary life does here on earth.

Fear God and Keep His Commandments

The wise man, Solomon, recommended that instead of spending our time on earth chasing the wind and chasing after vanity, we should be most concerned with fearing God and keeping his commandments. Let us take a moment to digest that statement.

It said, first to *"Fear God"*. The word *"fear"* in this context connotes *being afraid of what something is capable of doing. It is a fear that means to approach with great respect.* It is like the fear we have of high voltage. When you approach or interact with high voltage, you approach it cautiously with fear and great respect. You do not dare approach it irresponsibly or in a careless way unless you are plain stupid, or it is your weapon of choice for committing suicide.

God is far more powerful and deadly than high voltage, and when you approach or deal with God, you must recognize his awesomeness. High voltage is a good thing when it is providing electrical energy to power our homes and businesses. However, that same high voltage can turn you into crispy burnt toast if you mishandle it. Therefore, to fear God is to have awe and respect for Him and realize He is nothing to play with.

Then Solomon added to *"fear God"*, one must also *"keep His Commandments"*. The word *"keep"* in this context means *to obey or do what the commandments command.* God lets us know by the Word of God, that if we do not obey His Commandments, we will suffer consequences and ultimately garner His judgment and eternal punishment. In addition, keeping His commandments demonstrates and validates that you in fact love God. For it is written, *"If you love me, keep my commandments"*. John 14:15

The Difference between God and High Voltage

The unmistakable difference between God and high voltage is clear and simple. God is merciful, gracious, and forgiving, and high voltage is not. If you mishandle high voltage, it will immediately knock your lights out and usher you into the next life (No questions asked). However, if you disrespect God by disobeying Him, He is likely to temporarily ignore your stupidity and act as if He did not see what you did. He will give you an opportunity to right your wrong, only because He is a loving and merciful God.

Nevertheless, keep this point in mind also. God is not fooled, nor can you make a fool of Him. Whatsoever evil deeds you sow, you will reap in due season. Whatever you sow, (good or bad) will eventually return to you in some form. If you do not receive that reaping in this life, surely it will show up on your doorstep in the life to come.

The Bible - The Most Reliable Information Source for Life

The Bible is a micro-library of many books that tells the story of the love relationship between God and man. It gives us a historical and futuristic account of how life as we know it began, what has unfolded over the course of time, what will happen in the future, and how it will all end.

The first chapter of the Bible reveals what God created in the beginning. It is a journal of what happened on each day of creation, and the vision God had in mind for man.

The second chapter describes the paradise state of the earth before the fall of man and sets the stage for what caused man to interrupt his harmonious relationship with God.

The third chapter reveals what went wrong and what caused hell to be unleashed on the earth and caused man to sever his harmonious relationship with God.

The last chapter of the Bible shows us how things were intended to be and what the final outcome will be.

All the rest of the books and their chapters in the Bible are intended to help man understand where he messed up, why he keeps messing up, how to get back on track, and how to get his act together and stay on track.

There are those who feel that the Bible cannot be totally trusted because man wrote it. What does not make rational sense to me is that these same people who do not fully trust the Bible because they believe it was written by man trust other books that were also written by, (you guessed it) man. Hypothetically, if an angel or alien wrote a book, as some believe and argue, how do they know that they can trust that angel or alien?

The claim of the Bible is that the Bible's information source is God, and God used holy men of God as instruments to put the information into written form. Nevertheless, some feel that man still tampered with the Word when it was translated. Technically what they are implying is that the God who created this extraordinarily vast and complex universe and maintains an orderly and consistent operation of that universe is not capable of preventing humans from tampering with His Word.

Even if it were possible for man to have altered the Word of God, I do not know of any other information source that has stood the same test of time, is packed with its plethora of current relevant information, and has countless prophecies that have been fulfilled to the "T".

Nevertheless, this book is not about proving the validity of the Bible, as I believe the Bible has already proved itself. The Bible offers us precise information that will prove to be true as well as beneficial and will change our lives for the better if we interpret it correctly and do what it tells us to do.

The Real Problem of Humanity

Genesis is the first book in the Bible, and the term means "origin" or beginning. Ironically, that is what the book does convey. It tells us how this world began and how sin entered this world. The first three chapters of Genesis are indeed the foundation for the rest of the Bible.

Once we get to the third chapter, all hell breaks loose. Adam seriously shatters the relationship between God and him. Adam was utterly incapable of doing what was required to make amends. Adam's flawed character became a hereditary disease. Adam's character defect has affected every generation of humans without exception. Adam's disease is a spiritual disease called sin, which affects the heart and moral character of every human being that descended from him.

Adam and every human since have been incapable of overcoming this disease. Therefore, God had to become a human, defeat the disease, and provide the vaccine to cure this infectious disease for the rest of us. The cure is the blood of Jesus. Now, through the acceptance of this vaccine and the recommended follow-up therapy, deliverance from this deadly disease is made possible.

After the third chapter of Genesis, the rest of the Bible deals with the protracted process of rectifying the same out-of-control spiritual pandemic. Even though the vaccine is readily available in abundance, many are still suffering and dying daily from the disease of sin and rebellion.

Once we get a clearer understanding of what happened in the third chapter of Genesis, we will see that history keeps repeating itself and incessantly so. We are still making the very same mistake Adam and Eve made. The devil is still using the same tricks on us today. It appears we are stuck on stupid because in spite of the fact that we have the record of Adam and Eve and others to learn from, we keep making the same error continually. It is very difficult to fix stupidity and insanity. That said, let us move on, and explore what happened in the beginning.

CHAPTER TWO
Pre-Creation And
The Creation of the World

Pre-Creation

God existed before the creation of anything. God is an eternal being, and He has neither beginning nor ending. He was not born, created, made, or evolved from anything else because there was nothing before Him. He is the Alpha and the Omega. He is the beginning and the end of all things created. He is the only non-created being ever in existence and He created and made everything that exists.

This concept is very difficult for humans to wrap their minds around because we think in terms of time. The concept of something not having a beginning reference point in time is virtually inconceivable to us. Nevertheless, God has no beginning and He will never die or cease to be.

Therefore, God was present before the heavens and the earth came into being. How long God existed before He decided to create the heavens and the earth is unknown, and unknowable. What we do know from the Word of God is that, *"In the beginning of creation, was the Word. The Word was with God and the Word was God". (**John 1:1**)* This entity called *the Word* is the primary source of all knowledge, information, and intelligence. God by His Word created everything that exists anywhere and everywhere.

God first created the invisible spiritual world before He created the visible physical world. He created thrones, powers, principalities, dominions, and an innumerable host of angelic beings. He established His throne and His place of abode, which is the Heaven of the heavens.

What Is Heaven?

Heaven is a spiritual environment characterized by pure peace, love, holiness, righteousness, and is devoid of all evil forces and elements. It is not a physical or a geographical place. It is *a place of spiritual awareness and holy righteous compliance.* In other words, it is a place where everything is acutely aware of God and His preeminent sovereignty, and they obey and carry out His Will always. Flesh and blood, physical matter, or anything unholy, cannot enter or exist in this environment. God only allows holy spiritual entities into His holy environment.

God created the physical heavens and the earth after establishing His invisible Kingdom of God in Heaven. He used things in the invisible world to make the things seen in the physical world. God had in mind the creation of an entity that was like Him. He wanted this entity to be a physical expression of Himself, a hardcopy of the invisible God. God desired to have a special love relationship with this physical expression of Himself. He called this expression, man. God did not want this love relationship to be a love relationship prompted by force or preprogramming, but one that developed by choice and based on mutual respect, trust, and commitment to one another.

It Takes Faith to Believe in God
From a human perspective, our relationship with God is similar to a blind date. We have never seen God. We have only heard about Him from others. Nevertheless, based on the words and testimony of individuals whom we have never met in person, we believe what they say about this invisible God and trust that every word said about Him is true.

This is the fundamental nature of faith. Faith is believing in something that you cannot see physically, but offers enough experiential and factual evidence to convince us that what we have heard about this God is true; moreover, we confidently put our trust in the Word of God. It is no different from the faith and trust we put in so many other things in our daily lives.

Some of us work for large companies but we have never seen the owner who promises to give us a paycheck for working every day. We also trust that the company is actually investing the money we place with it into our retirement plan. For the most part, we do not actually see the physical money; we just see a report of how much money is supposed to be in our account. We saw in 2001 what happened at Enron and how they fraudulently ripped off their employees and stockholders.

Nevertheless, we trust that what the company tells us is true. We even go out and buy houses, cars, and many other things on credit, trusting that we will have our jobs long enough to pay off the debt. Our paychecks and retirement funds can disappear overnight as we have also seen in recent years with other major companies.

We confidently get in cars every day and ride on roads and highways that we trust that will safely get us to where we are going. We do not really know whether these things are as safe as they say they are, but based on experiential and factual evidence, we trust our lives to these roads and to these vehicles. We trust in so many things that we cannot see, do not understand, and know little or nothing about. We trust that the sky is not going to fall on us, we trust that the ground is not going to open up and swallow us, and that the planets and stars are not going to suddenly fall from the heavens.

Although we cannot see God, we should have enough sense to realize that in the history of humankind those things with intelligent design and functionality required an intelligent source to make them happen.

Imagine if you will, someone creating an explosion. After the smoke cleared, what emerged as a result of the explosion was a Mac computer complete with an Apple logo and software. That is not likely to happen in a million years with a trillion attempts. Scientists need to stop tripping. They know stuff like that does not make any logical or scientific sense whatsoever.

The only way you would ever get intelligent design and functionality resulting from a single explosion is, if a very sophisticated being, a being like God created that explosion. Therefore, if the universe is the result of a big-bang explosion, God is the only being intelligent enough to have pulled off that explosion.

We know that the universe, humans, plants, and animals are highly sophisticated and complex entities. Man has never created or made anything with the same or greater capabilities as what God created. These things are way beyond the knowledge and comprehension of man. Therefore, some superior intelligence source had to be responsible for their creation.

Whether you believe that source is God or some other entity, it should be evident that whoever or whatever that source is, it has to be an extremely intelligent source. God is the One who is responsible for creating the heavens and the earth and the fullness thereof according to the

Bible. For those of you who do not believe this truth, that is precisely why the Bible says, ...*"The FOOL has said in his heart, there is no God..." (Psalms 53:1)* Do not get offended or angry with me, but the Bible does says that you are a fool if you say there is no God, and I agree with what the Bible says wholeheartedly, without apology or reservations.

The Beginning of Creation

The first words we find in the Bible as the story unfolds in *Genesis 1:1* are: *"In the beginning God created the heavens and the earth"*. This God whom Solomon said we should fear is the same God who created the heavens and the earth in the beginning. This first verse of Scripture is simply stating a fundamental fact. It is telling us who created **"what"** and **"when"**. God is the **"who"**, that created the heavens and the earth. The heavens and the earth is **"what"** He created, and in the beginning is **"when"** he did it.

"In the beginning" refers to the beginning of creation, not the beginning of time. I know that may sound a little strange to some, but let me explain. In *Genesis 1:1*, time does not exist. Time is a function of a continuous celestial clock cycle of the sun and the moon. The sun and the moon did not come into existence until the fourth day of creation. A cycle of evening and morning was what constituted a day, before the sun and moon were created.

The Difference between Day and day, and Night and night

To complicate this matter and confuse you even more, *Genesis 1:5*, reads, *"And God called the light Day, and the darkness he called Night. And the evening and the morning were the first day"* Notice that God called the light **"Day"** and the word is capitalized. Then God called the darkness **"Night"** and that is also capitalized. However, the sentence ends with the word **"day"** and that is not capitalized.

What this means is that there is a concept called light that is also called Day and there is, a concept called darkness that is also called Night. These two concepts are different from the concept of day and night, as we know them. If we review the last chapter of the Bible, we will better understand the difference between Day and day, and Night and night.

These verses described, the New Jerusalem, which will come down from Heaven. It says in *Revelation 21:23*, that *the city will not need the sun or the moon for light because the glory of God, will illuminate it.* Then *Reve-*

lation 22:5 states, that *there will be no night.*

The sun and moon that were made by God in *Genesis 1:16,* were made to give light to the earth during the day and night, respectively. However, we see in *Revelation 21:23,* that the sun and the moon have both been retired from their respective jobs, and their services are no longer needed. Nevertheless, the city still has light without the sun or moon being present.

Therefore, the light, called Day, in *Genesis 1:5,* is the same light that illuminates the New Jerusalem, in *Revelation 21:23*. The capitalized Day and Night, is a spiritual concept and the lower case day and night, is a concept of nature, based on the cycle of the sun and the moon, which were also created by God. (Are you confused yet? Great!)

To shed more light on this concept, consider, *"the Kingdom of Light"* vs. *"the Kingdom of Darkness"*. The Kingdom of Light is a concept wherein God is the supreme ruler and the Word of God, governs everything and is the ultimate, and thus the Eternal Light. Only good, holiness, and righteousness are present, and there is no darkness of any kind in this Kingdom. No form of darkness can exist in this environment because the Light expels all darkness.

The Kingdom of Darkness is a concept wherein Satan is the chief ruler, and everything is based on lies, deceptions, misinformation, and misconceptions. This kingdom is about keeping people from knowing the truth, the facts, and reality. This is what it means to be living in darkness or the Dark Age. Truth is hard to find, when darkness rules and false information is plentiful.

Truth is Light, and lies and deceptions are destroyed when Truth exposes them. People who are living according to the rules and standards of the world, live in darkness because they love the pleasures of sin and do not want to abandon those enjoyments.

The Light commands and demands us to repent of sinning and live instead holy and righteously. Only true believers are willing to live in the Light. Carnal-minded believers, religious people, and sinners prefer living in darkness. They regard the darkness more comfortable, less confrontational, and more fun loving. It does not conflict with their carnal and immoral desires and standards. It allows them to live however they want to live without submitting to or being challenged by God's standards.

The Concept of: The Evening and The Morning

The evening and the morning, in the context of the first chapter of Genesis, is a concept that relates to eternity. *Eternity* is a spiritual world environment concept that is timeless, and spaceless. In the realm of eternity, time does not exist, and it has no relevance.

The concept of having a beginning and end, is relative to time and space, but not eternity. It indicates that, there is a certain point in time, when something begins to exist or move, *(its beginning)* and a certain point in time, when it stops moving, or ceased to exist, *(its end)*. They are only **reference points,** used to distinguish, reveal, or measure how much time has elapsed, or where on the time continuum a particular event occurs.

For example: If you want to refer to a certain event that happened in the past, you would indicate that this event occurred on a certain day of a particular month and a particular year. This becomes the time reference point. However, there is no certain day, time, month, or year to reference in eternity.

The evening and the morning in *Genesis 1,* refers to an interval that God used to mark off what he designated as a day, during the creation age. During this age, God was moving things in His creation work environment from a state of darkness, to a state of light, from a state of non-existence, to a state of existence, and a state of chaos, to a state of order. There is no certain date reference, which can be assigned to these events. There is only a reference to, the six days of creation. There is no year and month, which references the six days of creation.

After these, six days, and the seventh day of rest that followed, God's work did not continue to the eighth day or the next week. It stopped there, because God had completed all of His intended creation work. There was nothing else, that He was going to personally create or make. After the six days of creation and the day of rest on the seventh day, the creation era clock, defined by what God called the evening and the morning, ended. Technically, the creation era, lasted only six creation workdays and the seventh day, was a pause between the completion of creation, and life being put in motion.

We have no Biblical information, that I know of, that tells us how long a creation day lasted in terms of time, as we understand it. One creation day could have been equivalent to a thousand years, a million years, or just ten minutes. That is something we do not know, and probably do not really need to know.

I personally do not know when the celestial clock, based on the continual cycle of the sun and moon, started ticking. I would imagine, that it started when Adam was created. I say that because the Bible tells us that Adam was the first man on earth, and the Bible tells us how many years he lived. If it says that he lived a certain number of years, then that means, that, the clock had to have started ticking about the time when he was created, in order to correspond with the number of years he actually lived.

On the other hand, the clock could have started as soon as God made the sun and moon, or shortly thereafter. However, it probably did not, because that was only the fourth day of creation, and there were yet three more days to go, on the creation clock. At that time, God was still calling a creation day, the evening, and the morning, which was His reference to a full day, during the creation period.

I really do not know and do not really care when the celestial clock started. What matters to me is that my name is written in the Lamb's Book of Life and that I will be found worthy to enter into his glorious Kingdom. Let the scientist wreck their brains trying to figure out all such complicated stuff and make up numbers that will impress those who want to make others think they know something deep and important. I do not have time to waste on such trivial and frivolous details.

Darkness Precedes Light

Note that in *Genesis 1:2*, darkness was mentioned before light.

Genesis 1:2 And **the earth** *was without form, and void; and* **darkness** *was upon the face of the deep. And the Spirit of God moved upon the face of the waters.*

Darkness is *the partial or total absence of light*. Darkness makes it difficult or even impossible to see or become aware or conscious of something or know and understand what that something is. It conceals and hides things and makes them obscure, so they cannot be perceived. In the beginning, this is how it was. Although there was something present, it was humanly impossible to see or know what was there because of the thick darkness that was there.

When we more closely examine *Genesis 1:2* above, we will find something else very interesting. In *Verse 2*, the first thing that is mentioned is the **earth**. It says, *"The earth was"*, but it did not have a defined shape or *form*. It did not say there was no earth, and then God created or made it. It says, **"it was"** (it existed already) without form. In *Genesis 1:1*, the Scripture told us that in the beginning of creation, God created the heavens and the earth. In *Genesis 1:2*, we see that the heavens and the earth that God created, had also been made, but they were obscured or hidden by the darkness and by the waters beneath that darkness.

Therefore, we see that before God introduced light, darkness was already present. If light was already present, there would have been no need for God to say, *"Let there be light"*. God always throughout the Bible and throughout history allows a dark period of existence to prevail before He introduces light.

After the dark period runs its course, then God sends forth light into the dark environment to expel the darkness and shed light on the current situation to bring order to the situation and rectify it. Light is not needed where sufficient light is already present. God had to let darkness overshadow humanity, so that humanity could see and understand why we needed the Son of God to bring us light.

Let There Be Light

Genesis 1:3 And God said, Let there be light: and there was light.

Genesis 1:4 And God saw the light, that it was good: and God divided the light from the darkness.

In Genesis 1:2, God had already made the heavens and the earth, but what He had made was not visible because of the darkness, because of the vastness of the waters, and because everything was in disarray and indistinguishable. There was no space, light, or boundaries set as yet to distinguish one thing from another. These concepts had not yet been introduced and applied to God's newly created world.

In *Verse 3* of *Genesis 1*, we find that the first words God uttered was, "Let there be Light". When God turned on the Light, that is the revealing moment when we begin to realize that God had already made something. Initially, before He turned on the Light, we had no clue as to what was there because the thick darkness totally concealed it. It was not until God introduced Light that it was possible to see that there was something there besides darkness. We thus discovered that there was an immeasurable amount of water underneath the thick darkness.

Light is the exact opposite of darkness. It is defined as *the natural agent that stimulates sight and makes things visible.* Light is *anything that makes manifest, reveals, or illuminates whatever is present.*

Accurate knowledge and information is spiritual light. Wrong or inaccurate information is a form of spiritual darkness. The Word of God is accurate and reliable information. It makes those things that pertain to life and godliness known to us. When we have the knowledge of God, we can see clearly how to live a righteous life that is pleasing to God.

Light makes it possible to know, understand, discern, and distinguish one thing from another. It allows us to identify what something is and is not. Therefore, once the light was present, it expelled the darkness and enabled us to see and make sense of what was there all the time, but hidden by the darkness.

When the light appeared, the darkness that was obscuring the visibility of the components of creation had to immediately vacate the premises, so that what God had made could be revealed. The more information from God we introduce into our minds and put into regular practice, the more the dark evil and sinful things in our minds and hearts will vanish from our lives.

When God introduced light into the creation work environment, He set the first boundaries for that work, which separated and distinguished **light** from **darkness**. Once the light was introduced into the work environment, the darkness disappeared from the face of the waters. The light made it possible to see the waters. The physical heavens, the earth, and the seas were situated under the vastness of water, patiently waiting to be discovered.

The Introducing of Space

Space is *the concept of separation.* Space *makes it possible to distinguish one thing from another.* In the absence of space, nothing can have a definable shape or form. Without space, everything that is present is jumbled together and has the appearance of chaos. If the very words on your screen or paper that you are reading were devoid of all space, it would be impossible for you to read this book. You would not be able to distinguish the letters and the words.

That is why in the beginning, the earth did not have any form or shape because you could not distinguish it from the waters. However, when God introduced space by separating the waters from the waters and creating the firmament and commanding the seas to gather together;

He define each component's space, which is what made it possible to distinguish the seas from the earth and the earth from the sky.

If you took everything in your house, stacked it all in one room, and made the room pitch dark, it would be impossible to see what was sitting in that room without introducing a light source. Once you introduce light into the room, you would be able to see that something was in the room, but it might be still difficult to identify what exactly was in the room because it was all jumbled together.

However, if you pull everything out of the room and give each item its own designated space, you could then clearly distinguish and identify each item. This is how it was in the beginning. God had to bring in the light and give everything its own space and form. Then and only then was it possible to see what God had created and indeed had already made.

Genesis 1:6 And God said, Let there be a firmament in the midst of the waters, and let it divide the waters from the waters.

Genesis 1:7 And God made the firmament, and divided the waters which were under the firmament from the waters which were above the firmament: and it was so.

Genesis 1:8 And God called the firmament Heaven. And the evening and the morning were the second day.

In Genesis 1:6, God introduced space. The firmament was the sky and outer space. This firmament separated the waters. Some of the waters were suspended above the firmament, and some remained below the firmament. At this stage of unveiling what God had created and made, the earth was still covered by the waters below the firmament, and that led to God making his next move.

Revealing the Earth

Genesis 1:9 And God said, Let the waters under the heavens be gathered together unto one place, and let the dry land appear: and it was so.

Genesis 1:10 And God called the dry land Earth; and the gathering together of the waters called he Seas: and God saw that it was good.

In order for God to reveal the Earth that He had already made, He commanded the waters that were covering the Earth, to recede and back off the land so that the earth could be recognized and seen. Notice that the earth was there already. It was only a matter of uncovering it. It was as if God made the earth and then threw a thick blanket of water over it to conceal it.

At that time, the waters that formed the seas were gathered together in one place. At some point in time, the landmass apparently separated causing an ocean of water to form between the Eastern and the Western continents.

The Order of the Unveiling of Creation
Notice the order God used to introduce each component of His creation. First, He turned on the Light to make things visible in the eternity work environment. Then He created living environments and spaces for the various life forms to live in. Then He created two great celestial lamps (the sun and the moon) to determine time, the seasons, days, and years and give light to the earth. Then He populated the living environments with life forms. After having done all of that, He created and made man to rule over every living creature on the earth.

Also, notice that God in His infinite wisdom, did not make man first. He made him last. If God had made man first, man would have believed and thus acted as if man created everything, or constantly would have tried to tell God, what God should do and how He should do it. Thankfully, when man came on the scene, everything was already there. Therefore, man could not patent or take credit for what God had already made.

When God created all the other life forms, He simply spoke to the waters and the earth and commanded them to bring forth the appropriate life forms. But when it came to man, God spoke to Himself, and said, *"Let us make man in our image, after our likeness: and let them have dominion over the fish of the sea, and over the fowl of the air, and over the cattle, and over all the earth, and over every creeping thing that creepeth upon the earth"*. **Genesis 1:26**

***Genesis 1:27** So God created man in his own image, in the image of God created he him; male and female created he them.*

***Genesis 1:28** And God blessed them, and God said unto them, Be fruitful, and multiply, and replenish the earth, and subdue it: and have dominion over the fish of the sea, and over the fowl of the air, and over every living thing that moveth upon the earth.*

Man Has a Special Relationship with God
Here is where the story gets quite interesting. Up until now, God was

only dealing with things that had a creational relationship with God. The sun, the moon, the stars, vegetation, and the animals do not have an intimate love relationship with God. In fact, all things that God made before he made man were created to benefit man in some way. From God's point of view, man was the most prized creation of all of God's creations. Man was the only creation of God's that God gave such high and extraordinary honor and glory; not even the angels had such status. Indeed, even they were created in part to serve man.

God created animals and vegetation to be used and consumed. As we can read, in Old Testament times, animals were killed daily and offered as a sacrifice. Conversely, God regarded the life of humans as sacred.

Genesis 9:2 And the fear of you and the dread of you shall be upon every beast of the earth, and upon every fowl of the air, upon all that moveth upon the earth, and upon all the fishes of the sea; into your hand are they delivered.

3 Every moving thing that liveth shall be meat for you; even as the green herb have I given you all things.

4 But flesh with the life thereof, which is the blood thereof, shall ye not eat.

5 And surely your blood of your lives will I require; at the hand of every beast will I require it, and at the hand of man; at the hand of every man's brother will I require the life of man.
6 Whoso sheddeth man's blood, by man shall his blood be shed: for in the image of God made he man.

So we see from these verses that God made a big distinction between animal life and human life. He states in *Genesis 9:5* that *"if anyone kills a human, be it man or beast, the same shall be put to death"*. That is how special human life is to God. He made this law concerning the life of humans because humans were made in the image of God, thus indicating that there was no other creature with the same designation.

There is no other creature that God refers to as a son of God. There is no other creature that He sent his Son to die for other than man. The angels are only servants of God. Humans are designated as joint heir with Christ to be rulers of the Kingdom of God on Earth. These are special designations only granted to humans.

God Created Everything with a Clear Purpose in Mind

Isaiah 45:18 For thus saith the LORD that created the heavens; God himself that formed the earth and made it; he hath established it, he created it not in vain, he formed it to be inhabited: I am the LORD; and there is none else.

Isaiah 45:7 *I form the light, and create darkness: I make peace, and create evil: I the LORD do all these things.*

Colossian 1:16 *For by him were all things created, that are in heaven, and that are in earth, visible and invisible, whether they be thrones, or dominions, or principalities, or powers: all things were created by him, and for him:*

Romans 9:17 *For the Scripture saith unto Pharaoh, Even for this same purpose have I raised thee up, that I might show my power in thee, and that my name might be declared throughout all the earth.*

Before I go further, I want to clear up what is said in *Isaiah 45:7* about **God creating evil**. What that passage means is that evil and sin are virtually synonymous. Sin is the transgression or breaking of the Law. Therefore, once God instituted His Law and made it effective, by definition and by default it created the prospects of sin and evil also occurring. If you take away the Law, then there is nothing to say that you are doing something wrong or evil. However, once the Law goes into effect, anything that you do that violates or transgresses that Law is now considered sin and thus evil.

In addition, you must understand the purpose of creating such a designation. The Law is a good thing and was created to show us what is right and pleasing to God. Sin and evil were created to punish the lawbreakers, not the law obeyers. Just as it is with the law of the land, if I obey the laws, I have no need to fear the police. However, if I am a lawbreaker, then I have to watch out for the police because their job is to arrest me if I am caught breaking the law.

God created the earth as an environment for humans and other life forms of nature to live. Heaven is an environment where spirit beings live. Yet, God created man as a physical being and made a physical environment for him called earth. God's objective is to bring the concept of Heaven and the Kingdom of God eternally down to earth. Man's soul, which is spiritual and invisible, can temporarily go to Heaven when he dies if man has made the appropriate reservations. In the end, however, he will be returning to earth to spend eternity. This is the whole purpose of the resurrection and the transformation of the saints.

Who Is Us?

Going back to ***Genesis 1:26***, God said, *"Let us make man in our image, after our likeness: and let them have dominion over the fish of the sea, and over the* *fowl of the air, and over the cattle, and over all the earth, and over every creeping thing that creepeth upon the earth".*

Notice that God said, **"let us"**. Who is this **"us"**? This "us" is God the Father and God the Son. Jesus said, *"I and my Father are one". (John 10:30)*

John 14:8 *Philip saith unto him, Lord, show us the Father, and it sufficeth us.*

John 14:9 *Jesus saith unto him, Have I been so long time with you, and yet hast thou not known me, Philip? He that hath seen me hath seen the Father; and how sayest thou then, show us the Father?*

John 1:1 *In the beginning was the Word, and the Word was with God, and the Word was God.*

John 1:14 *And the Word was made flesh, and dwelt among us, (and we beheld his glory, the glory as of the only begotten of the Father,) full of grace and truth.*

The above Scriptures make it very clear who "us" is. In the beginning, the Word was with God and the Word was God, and that same Word that was God and with God is the Word that became flesh (a human being), which was Jesus, the Son of God. Therefore, the Father and the Son is one God assuming two different roles.

God the Father fulfills the role of creator and sustainer of the universe, and God the Son is the Savior of the world. God the Father is the Source, and God the Son is the Way, to connect to the Source. God is the only being in existence that can fulfill both roles.

I know here that some of you are asking about the Holy Spirit. The Father and the Son is the Holy Spirit. The Holy Spirit is the complete Spirit of God. God is a spirit being and God is the Spirit of Love. Jesus is the Spirit of Truth. These two Spirits are one Spirit, which is the Holy or complete Spirit of God. Therefore, the Father and the Son equal the Holy Spirit.

Understanding the Godhead

The Godhead consists of the Father, the Son, and the Holy Spirit. The Father and the Son are **family-related terms** that reflect how members of a family unit relate to one another. The father is the source or seed from which the son is produced. The son is a reflection and the product or offspring of the source seed of the father.

Every seed produces an extension and revelation of its own fundamental characteristics and nature. In other words, what is programmed in the source seed is decoded or revealed in the fruit produced from that source seed. The tree or offspring then produces and reveals the mystery that was hidden in the source seed.

What Is the Spirit of God?

The Spirit is not a family-related term. The Spirit is **a term that relates to form and power**. It relates to a **form of life** or a **form of existence**. The Spirit is also the power source for all living creatures. The Spirit of God is both God's form of **Existence** and His **Power**.

The Spirit of God is characterized and empowered by two spiritual powers. Power is the ability, strength, and capacity to do something. What the Spirit has the ability to produce is (Love Fruits)

Galatians 5:22 But the fruit of the Spirit is love, joy, peace, longsuffering, gentleness, goodness, faith, meekness, and temperance.

What the Spirit has the ability to communicate is (Truth) The Spirit of God produces and demonstrates the attributes of Love and communicates Truth. Love and Truth are the essence of the power of Almighty God.

John 15:26 NLT "But I will send you the Advocate—the Spirit of truth. He will come to you from the Father and will testify all about me.

John 16:13 NLT When the Spirit of truth comes, he will guide you into all truth. He will not speak on his own but will tell you what he has heard. He will tell you about the future.

1 John 4:6 NLT But we belong to God, and those who know God listen to us. If they do not belong to God, they do not listen to us. That is how we know if someone has the Spirit of truth or the spirit of deception.

When we obey the Word of Truth that the Spirit of Truth communicates to our spirit, that Word will produce the fruit of the Spirit in our hearts. Those love fruits produced in our hearts will flow out of our being in the form of words and deeds of life and demonstrations of acts of love. When we walk in love, we walk in the Spirit. When we walk in the Spirit, we walk in unity and harmony with God. When we walk in unity and harmony with God, we become one with God and reflect the image of God.

The son is the Truth, and Jesus declared, taught, and demonstrated the Truth. He showed us the way back to the Father who is Love. He showed us the lifestyle that pleases the Father. This is why he was able to make the claim of being the Way, the Truth, and the Life.

John 14:6 *Jesus saith unto him, I am the way, the truth, and the life: no man cometh unto the Father, but by me.*

Two Roles, One God, One Power Source

Therefore, The Godhead is the Father and the Son, identical in nature and character but different in terms of their roles in the story of life. They are one Spirit. The Holy Spirit is both the Father and the Son. It is God, playing both family roles.

John 10:30 *I and my Father are one.*

John 14:8 NLT *Philip said, "Lord, show us the Father, and we will be satisfied."*

John 14:9 NLT *Jesus replied, "Have I been with you all this time, Philip, and yet you still don't know who I am? Anyone who has seen me has seen the Father! So why are you asking me to show him to you?*

Jesus was clearly declaring himself as God. God is the Father, and Jesus was telling Phillip when you see me, you are looking at the Father. The Father and the Son are the same person, and they both are God, powered by the Holy Spirit.

Ephesians 4:5 *There is one Lord, one faith, one baptism,*

Ephesians 4:6 *and one God and Father, who is over all and in all and living through all.*

The Father and the Son Both Exist Together as a Single Spirit Form

John 4:24 *God is a Spirit: and they that worship him must worship him in spirit and in truth.*

God is a spirit being. Spirit beings are by nature and design both invisible and intangible. However, they have the ability to transform into a physical tangible form or manifest their nature and character through physical objects and entities.

John 1:1 NIV *In the beginning was the Word, and the Word was with God, and the Word was God.*

John 1:2 NIV *He was with God in the beginning.*

***John 1:14** NIV The Word became flesh and made his dwelling among us. We have seen his glory, the glory of the one and only Son, who came from the Father, full of grace and truth.*

The Son, which is the Word (the Spirit of Truth) temporarily took on a human form to enable humans to see what God looks like and how He behaves in a human format. This format served as a visual example and a model of what God intended for humans to be like. He also took on this form to represent all of humanity at the cross, defeat sin through his righteous living, and conquer death and hell through his death, resurrection, and ascension. In so doing, Jesus pre-qualifies everyone to be recipients of salvation and have access to the resources of the Kingdom of God. (I just said, a mouthful)

Since we know that God is a Spirit Being, and Jesus the Son is the Truth. We know that the Truth is the Word of God and that Word, is God. That means that the Son, who is also the Word, is also, a Spirit Being, the same as is the Father. God, is a Spirit, and God is Love, which makes Him, the Spirit of Love. Jesus is the Word of Truth, which is the Spirit of Truth. Therefore, the two Spirits, are united as a single Spirit that reflects the complete and perfect Spirit of God, called the Holy Spirit.

***1John 4:8** NIV Whoever does not love does not know God, because God is love.*

***1John 4:16** NIV And so we know and rely on the love God has for us. God is love. Whoever lives in love lives in God, and God in them.*

CHAPTER THREE
The Creation of Man

Made In the Image and the Likeness of God

Now that we understand who the "us" is, we need to understand the other part of the statement, which is *"Make man in our image, after our likeness"*.

Genesis 1:26 *And God said, Let us make man in our image, after our likeness: and let them have dominion over the fish of the sea, and over the fowl of the air, and over the cattle, and over all the earth, and over every creeping thing that creepeth upon the earth.*

God created man in His image, which reflects His character and after His likeness, which emulate his abilities, behavior, and deeds. God created man to be just as He is and having the same nature, quality, temperament, persona, spirit, and moral fiber. In other words, God intended man to emulate Him, rather than act like the devil or nonregenerated man.

A character when related to a story is a person or personality that plays a certain role in a story. That role defines that character and dictates how he will essentially act and behave. So likewise, your character dictates your behavior. For example, if someone was playing the role of a corrupt politician in a movie, that role will set the tone and nature of that particular character.

God Created Man to Be Like Himself

Man was created by God to be like him in character and capability. Man is the only creation on earth that is able to communicate using sophisticated words and expressions. He is the only species that can create new and different things and experiences. All other creatures are limited to instinctive behavior. They keep doing the same thing from generation to generation.

None of the other species wears clothes that they can make for themselves. They cannot cook food or process raw material to create new and innovative products. They cannot build structures beyond what they build instinctively. They cannot fly airplanes or drive cars. Only man has the ability to create new and innovative inventions. Therefore, man is potentially capable of doing anything God is capable of doing. This is true because God indicated that when humanity is unified, nothing is impossible, and indeed, all things are possible to those that believe.

Genesis 11:6 And the LORD said, "Behold, they are one people, and they have all one language, and this is only the beginning of what they will do. And nothing that they propose to do will now be impossible for them.

Psalm 82:6 I have said, Ye [are] gods; and all of you [are] children of the most High.

John 10:34 Jesus answered them, Is it not written in your law, I said, Ye are gods?

Mathew 17:20 And Jesus said unto them, Because of your unbelief: for verily I say unto you, If ye have faith as a grain of mustard seed, ye shall say unto this mountain, Remove hence to yonder place; and it shall remove; and nothing shall be impossible unto you.

Mark 9:23 Jesus said unto him, If thou canst believe, all things [are] possible to him that believeth.

Philippians 4:13 I can do all things through Christ which strengtheneth me.

God Has a Desire to Share Love

God is Love, but what is Love without someone to love and share it with? When God created man, He saw that it was not good for man to be alone. Adam was not necessarily lonely but he was alone in the sense that there was no other species compatible with him and like him.

Genesis 2:18 And the LORD God said, [It is] not good that the man should be alone; I will make him a help meet for him.

In order to share love in a meaningful way, God created man to be like Him. He created a physical representation of Himself that could have a family of sons and daughters to love and be loved by. This love relationship is what drives God to do the things He does. Love does not produce harmful effects. Love strives to produce good for everyone. Love protects those that abide in Love, and restrains and destroys those who refuse to abide in Love.

Man Is a Physical Expression of God

Man was created to be a physical expression and manifestation of what the invisible God is like. In other words, if you drew what the invisible God would look like in a visible form, He would look and function as a man. Therefore, if you see a godly righteous man, like God referred to of Job, he would be an animated graphical image of God.

However, when man sinned, that original image was disfigured and distorted. It still had some resemblance to God, but it no longer reflected all the corresponding qualities of God. Man began to be morphed into a combined hybrid image; a cross image of God and Satan. He continued to maintain some abilities of God, such as the ability to think, decide, create, and make, but he also took on the character of Satan and began to act and behave like a sinner and a rebel.

Man's dramatic image change was in effect like a sex or gender change. It was like being born a male and later changed into a female. A sex change redefines who you are and what you are. It changes your role and behavior. Instead of being and acting like a man, you begin to act like a woman. The original image has been reconfigured, distorted, which makes it difficult to determine whether the new image is the original or the morphed version.

In comparison, this is how it is with man. It is difficult to see the image of God clearly in humans because the image has been altered. When we see humans killing and hurting one another maliciously, this act does not reflect the character and behavior of God. Instead, it reproduces the character and behavior of the devil.

The Original Role of Man

The original role of man was to produce fruits of righteousness, multiply them on the earth, and fill the earth with righteous works and deeds. Conversely, the devil came to steal, kill, and destroy. When humans switched roles and began to do what Satan is famous for, we took on the role and character of the devil.

Humans tend to eat from the Tree of Knowledge of Good and Evil and consequently produce good and evil. God intended for man to produce good only. Nevertheless, because man has chosen to act in accordance with his own will and intellect, he produces hit and miss results. This is why sin is referred to as missing the mark. The bullseye is love and when we do evil, we miss the target. However, when we obey God's Word consistently, we always hit the bullseye, which is love.

Man can only consistently reflect the image of God by consistently obeying what God commands. Man must discipline himself to reject and cast out every thought and spirit that is contrary to God's principles, precepts, and every idea that attempts to supersede the knowledge of God. The more we learn of God's ways and then practice them daily, the more we will become like God. The superimposed image of the devil will begin to dissolve and fade away, and the clear image of God will re-emerge in its glory. We will again look and be like God.

Adam Was Originally Created as a Bi-Gender Being

Genesis 1:27 So God created man in his own image, in the image of God created he him; male and female created he them.

Genesis 5:2 Male and female created he them; and blessed them, and called their name Adam, in the day when they were created.

When God originally created Adam, he was both male and female. Notice that in *Verse 5:2* above, *He called their name "Adam"*. He did not call them *"Adam and Eve"* or the *"Adam family"*. Eve was originally in Adam. At that time, God recognized him as a single person with two genders (male and female). No, he was not a hermaphrodite. He did not have a male and a female sex organ, but he did possess both genders meaning he had both masculine and feminine qualities (I don't mean being gay-like or on the down-low).

The masculine part of man dominates and rules, but the feminine part of man submits, obeys, and assists. Man was created to rule over the earth and his own household. He can only do that effectively by submitting to God through Christ. Man was designated to be the head and spiritual covering for his wife, and at the same time, man must submit willfully to his own head and covering which is Christ.

This is why when God made woman, he put the man as head over her and commanded that wives, are to submit to their own husbands. Moreover, this is why He made the woman to be a helpmate, to assist the man in fulfilling God's ordained responsibilities. Woman is uniquely equipped and endowed to help man meet or achieve his God mandate.

When God put Adam to sleep, He extracted the female part of Adam and from Adam, he fashioned a seriously fine woman. Therefore, the one person (Adam) became physically two persons (Adam and Eve).

When two individual people (male and female) get married, the two become one spiritually, although they remain two physically. This is the same concept I explained earlier to explain the Father and the Son. They began as one, they became two separate entities with different roles, purposes, and identities, and then when the mission of the Son was accomplished, they became one Spirit again (The Holy Spirit).

Be Fruitful and Multiply

Genesis 1:28 And God blessed them, and God said unto them, Be fruitful, and multiply, and replenish the earth, and subdue it: and have dominion over the fish of the sea, and over the fowl of the air, and over every living thing that moveth upon the earth.

In the above verse, we see God placing man in control and giving him power over all animated living creatures. First, he gave Adam and Eve the command to be fruitful and to multiply. To be fruitful, means to produce much fruit or offspring. To multiply, implies increasing exceedingly and replenishing, means to fill up.

Therefore, God was commanding them to have children and to exceedingly increase the number of offspring, by their children having children and their children's children having children, until the earth was filled with people. God intended for the earth to be filled with an innumerable host of people.

When God told man to be fruitful and to multiply, on the surface, that meant for man to reproduce his biological seed and multiply it as I explained above. However, God was not just interested in having the earth filled with people. We see in *Genesis 6* before the flood that man had greatly increased in population, but those people had also greatly increased in wickedness and evil works. In spite of that multitude of people that had multiplied and filled the earth, God was sorely displeased because the people were wicked and evil. He desired a righteous generation.

Therefore, God was not just interested in large numbers of people. He was most interested in the earth being populated with righteous living people. God would rather have a few righteous people on earth, than a great multitude of wicked rebellious evildoers. He demonstrated this view with Sodom and Gomorrah. He destroyed these cities because of their sinful wicked living and lifestyles. He would have spared the cities if He could have found as few as ten righteous people in them.

Genesis 18:32 *And he said, Oh let not the Lord be angry, and I will speak yet but this once: Peradventure ten shall be found there. And he said, I will not destroy it for ten's sake.*

Abraham negotiated with God, starting with a proposal to spare the city, if 50 righteous people could be found in the city down to 10. What God was showing us here, is for a small group of righteous people, He would withhold his judgment on a city filled with wicked people. But when a city is so wicked, that there are virtually no righteous people in it, the city is good for nothing in God's eyes and indeed fit for destruction.

That being the case, God not only wants man to be fruitful and multiply the human species, He wants man to produce righteous fruit and to be fruitful in terms of producing good deeds and works in abundance.

Why God Wants So Many People on Earth
One of the primary reasons why God wants so many people on earth is because He knew that so many will not obey him. He foresaw that many would be destroyed for being disobedient, many would be destroyed for lack of knowledge, and many would be led astray by temptations, trials, lies, and deceptions.

Throughout the history of God's attempts to save a group of people, He always initially saved a very large group of people, but then had to wipe out and disqualify the bulk of them for the reasons mentioned above. It was always a much smaller group called the remnant that actually remained with God and received what He promised them.

Jude 1:5 *I will therefore put you in remembrance, though ye once knew this, how that the Lord, having <u>saved the people</u> out of the land of Egypt, afterward <u>destroyed them that believed not.</u>*

Numbers 32:11 *Surely none of the men that came up out of Egypt, from twenty years old and upward, shall see the land which I sware unto Abraham, unto Isaac, and unto Jacob; because <u>they have not wholly followed me</u>:*

Joshua 5:6 *For the children of Israel walked forty years in the wilderness, till all the people that were men of war, which came out of Egypt, were consumed, because <u>they obeyed not the voice of the LORD</u>: unto whom the LORD swore that he* *would not show them the land, which the LORD swore unto their fathers that he would give us, a land that floweth with milk and honey.*

1 Corinthians 10:1 *Moreover, brethren, I would not that ye should be ignorant, how that <u>all our fathers were under the cloud</u>, and <u>all passed through the sea</u>;*

1 Corinthians 10:2 *And were <u>all baptized unto Moses</u> in the cloud and in the sea;*

1 Corinthians 10:3 *And did <u>all eat the same spiritual meat</u>;*

1 Corinthians 10:4 *And did <u>all drink the same spiritual drink</u>: for they drank of that spiritual Rock that followed them: and that Rock was Christ.*

1 Corinthians 10:5 *But <u>with many of them God was not well pleased</u>: for <u>they were overthrown in the wilderness.</u>*

Romans 9:27 *Esaias also cried concerning Israel, Though the number of the children of Israel be as the sand of the sea, <u>a remnant shall be saved</u>:*

The above verses clearly demonstrate that God will save a large group of people from destruction; however, if some in that select group <u>believe not</u>, <u>do not wholly follow God</u>, <u>do not obey the voice of the Lord</u>, or <u>do not please God</u>, they <u>shall be eliminated from the saved group and destroyed</u>. Therefore, salvation without transformation leads to condemnation, and the judgment and destruction of the body, soul, and spirit.

The parable of the net alludes to this same outcome in ***Mathew 13:47***

Again, the kingdom of heaven is like unto a net, that was cast into the sea, and gathered of every kind:

Mathew 13:48 *Which, when it was full, they drew to shore, and sat down, and gathered the good into vessels, but cast the bad away.*

People of all kinds confess salvation and join a church. The church represents the net. However, many of the people in the church continue to live ungodly and worldly lifestyles. They represent the bad fish. Conversely, some people in the church do disconnect themselves from chasing after worldly and ungodly lusts and sincerely strive to live according to the Word of God. They represent the good fish. So as the parable illustrates, the bad fish will be cast away and the good fish will remain.

Mathew 7:19 *Every tree that bringeth not forth good fruit is hewn down, and cast into the fire.*

Mathew 7:20 Wherefore by their fruits ye shall know them.

Mathew 7:21 Not every one that saith unto me, Lord, Lord, shall enter into the kingdom of heaven; but he that doeth the will of my Father which is in heaven.

Mathew 7:22 Many will say to me in that day, Lord, Lord, have we not prophesied in thy name? and in thy name have cast out devils? and in thy name done many wonderful works?

Mathew 7:23 And then will I profess unto them, I never knew you: depart from me, ye that work iniquity.

What Are We Gonna Eat?

After God created man and gave him directives concerning his power and authority and his primary mission, Adam was getting hungry and wondered, what is for lunch? God knowing all his thoughts responded and said, *Behold, I have given you every herb bearing seed, which is upon the face of all the earth, and every tree, in the which is the fruit of a tree yielding seed; to you it shall be for meat.* **(Genesis 1:29)**

Genesis 1:30 And to every beast of the earth, and to every fowl of the air, and to every thing that creepeth upon the earth, wherein there is life, I have given every green herb for meat: and it was so.

In the beginning, both man and beast were restricted to a vegetarian diet. Humans were instructed to eat only seed-bearing herbs and the fruit of trees that produced a seed. All the land creatures and fowls were to eat only green herbs. God made no mention of what sea or water creatures should eat. However, after the flood in **Genesis 9:3**, God added meat to man's diet.

God then looked at all he had created and God saw every thing that he had made, and, behold, it was very good. And the evening and the morning were the sixth day. **(Genesis 1:31)**

God had worked diligently for six days unveiling and setting up the heavens, the earth, the seas, the inhabitants thereof, and their food provisions. He then took a deep breath, wiped the sweat from His forehead, and said, *"Man, I am tired, I need some rest"*. Therefore, instead of getting out of bed the next day to do more work, He stayed in bed, and thus on the seventh day, God rested.

Putting humor aside, God of course was not so exhausted from hard work that He needed to lie down and rest. Rest here, implies that God has finished His work. It means that on the seventh day, God did not do any more work because all the work He had set out to accomplish was finished. Rest is like retirement. It means you are ending your work career. God had completed creating everything He wanted to make, so subsequently, He retired from a career of creation and prepared to enter the salvation business. He foreknew that the first Adam was going to fail.

CHAPTER FOUR
Peace on Earth
In The Garden of Eden

God Reviewed His Work

In *Chapter 2 of Genesis,* God gives a very concise review of His creative work. This review gives us the basic details for how God created Adam and placed him in a special environment called the Garden of Eden. It goes on to tell us about the trees in this garden and gives us details of where this place called Eden was located. The Garden of Eden is a mysterious subject.

Genesis 2:8 And the LORD God planted a garden eastward in Eden; and there he put the man whom he had formed.

As I was writing this book, I explored what others have had to say about the physical and geographical location of Eden and the Garden of Eden. Some say it was near where Iran is, some say near Babylon, others say near Turkey. One even suggested Jerusalem. (Humorously, that looks like: *I ran to Babylon to get a Turkey to take back to Jerusalem?*) (LOL)

If I had to choose one of these, I would go with Jerusalem. The reason is that God has always made Jerusalem His fondest place. In the Old Testament, God chose Jerusalem as the place to build His holy temple. We also see the city of Jerusalem coming down from Heaven at the very end when the earth is restored to peace and righteousness. The very name Jerusalem also means "city of peace".

Canaan Is the Promised Land

Genesis 17:8 And I will give unto thee, and to thy seed after thee, the land wherein thou art a stranger, all the land of Canaan, for an everlasting possession; and I will be their God.

Canaan is the land that God promised to give to the seed of Abraham as their everlasting inheritance. This was a land flowing with milk and honey. What Canaan and Eden had in common were, they both are fertile and fruitful places, rich in resources, and possibly the most prime piece of real estate on earth. I also recognize there was a place call Eden, and there was a garden in Eden. Eden I believe was indeed a physical geographical location.

The garden however, may or may not be a precise physical geographical location. It may be a metaphoric and symbolic garden, or it may be both. Just as Canaan later became Israel, Eden may have become Canaan after the great flood in the days of Noah.

However, it is questionable whether or not this garden was an actual physical place on earth or a spiritual metaphor. According to the description of its location, it appears to be a physical location on earth. But if it is, where is this place now? No one has been able to pinpoint its location, and that is a bit strange. And if Adam and Eve were kicked out of it and angels with swords were set in place to prevent any unauthorized entry, it seems we should be able to at least see this place if it truly exists, even if we cannot enter it.

Perhaps the actual garden was destroyed in the flood, which is a reasonable explanation for what happened. Still the place called Eden is most likely still around under a new name. Perhaps some of the geographical characteristics identified in *Genesis* were also altered by the flood, thus making it difficult to pinpoint its location in the present day.

Was the Garden of Eden, a Physical Place, or a Spiritual Concept?

The fact that Adam and Eve were placed in the garden, gives us the impression that the Garden of Eden was a physical geographical location. However, being placed in a garden can also have spiritual implications. The Garden could be alluding to a spiritual environment, if we view it from a spiritual metaphorical perspective. The Garden of Eden was indeed, a special well protected and resource rich environment. It reminds me of what was said about *Job in Verse* **1:10 of Job**.

In *Job Verse 10*, we see that God had placed a spiritual wall of protection surrounding Job. Also, notice that Satan could not get to Job, without obtaining permission from God. Once God gave Satan permission to do whatever he wanted to Job, Satan had extensive access to Job.

Job 1:10 *Hast not thou made an hedge about him, and about his house, and* *about all that he hath on every side? thou hast blessed the work of his hands, and his substance is increased in the land.*

I believe Eden was *a place of spiritual protection* and provision. Spiritually speaking, it is *a place of obedience*. As long as we obey God and walk in His statutes as Job did, the devil cannot harm or persecute us *without God's permission*. If God grants the devil permission, it is only to prove that we are who and what God says we are or to strengthen and perfect us. Indeed, there are only four ways for Satan to gain access to a believer.

1. By permission from God; 2. By deception and trickery; 3. By our own consent or willful acceptance; and 4. By getting a believer to disobey God as Satan so skillfully did with Adam and his lovely wife.

Another key element that leads me to believe that Eden was a spiritual metaphor is **Genesis 3:24** says, *So he drove out the man; and he placed at the east of the garden of Eden Cherubims, and a flaming sword which turned every way, to keep the way of the tree of life.*

Notice that Cherubims were placed at the east of the garden to keep the way of the Tree of Life. The Tree of Life and the Tree of Knowledge of Good and Evil are two other mysterious objects or concepts in this passage of Scripture. No one has ever identified these trees as being literal physical trees, existing anywhere on earth. There is no mention of these trees being taken from earth either. The reason is that, both are spiritual metaphors.

If the Tree of Life is still in the garden and angels are assigned to protect it, and if it is a metaphoric or symbolic tree, then that indicates that the Garden of Eden also is symbolic. Once I break down the two symbolic trees, it all may begin to make spiritual sense to you.

Two Trees In The Midst Of the Garden

Two symbolic trees were in the midst of the Garden of Eden. One was the Tree of Life and the other was the Tree of Knowledge of Good and Evil. What should be rather obvious is that, the Tree of Life sounds like a tree that will give you life or cause you to live, and the Tree of Knowledge of Good and Evil, sounds like a tree, which will make you aware of good, but also evil things.

You might think this tree tells you clearly, what is good and what is evil. That is not how it works. It is a trial and error game. A thought comes to your mind, and you must decide whether to act on that thought or not. If you act on it, you will consequently learn from experience, whether that act was good or evil. But here is the kicker. Initially and maybe for a good while, it may seem like the act was good, but later on (Oh Boy! Gotcha!). All hell breaks out in your life, and you learn that, what you thought was good, turned out to be evil.

The Bible uses the metaphor of a tree to depict two different sources of knowledge. God chose this metaphor because a tree has many branches, and knowledge also has many branches. Further still, fruit trees produce food that nourishes the body. Comparatively, a metaphoric tree of knowledge can produce food that is nourishment for the mind.

One source of knowledge comes from the mind and the knowledge database of God and the other source (which is that of Satan) tends to take information from the database of God and distort, alter, twist, or pervert it, in an attempt to turn what is truth into a lie or turn what is a lie, into truth.

God gives humans free rein to decide which knowledge source they will use to retrieve their information. The choices are the Tree of Life (which produces righteous fruit and life everlasting) and the Tree of Knowledge of Good and Evil (which produces harm and death).

The Tree of Life symbolizes the Word of God, also referred to as the Word of Life and the Word of Truth. The Word of God provides us with reliable information to live a holy and righteous life that is acceptable to God. It produces life and everlasting life. The Tree of Life symbolizes, **obedience** to the Word of God and trusting wholeheartedly, what God says.

The Tree of Knowledge of Good and Evil symbolizes, humans leaning toward their own misguided intellectual understanding rather than trusting in what the Word of God says. It symbolizes **disobedience** to the Word of God. This misguided information comes from the devil, which suggests alternative ideas and solutions contrary to the Word of God. If God says you shall surely die, Satan suggests that God is lying, and emphatically declares that, you "shall not" surely die. This is Rule # 1 that you must know to overcome and defeat the devil.

RULE # 1: *Proverb 3:5 Trust in the LORD with all your heart; do not depend on your own understanding.*

God has all knowledge, wisdom, and understanding and all the answers, and He makes all the right decisions. Man's intelligence and the devil's intelligence are terribly limited and flawed. Which of the following two choices makes more sense: (A) To rely on, terribly flawed information or (B) To rely on, very accurate information?

(I really hope you are smart enough to answer this question correctly) However, in case you are not, I will give you the right answer. It is (B) The very accurate information. Unbelievably, Adam and Eve chose (A) and all the descendants of Adam at some point in time chose (A), also.

Here is the good news, however. Even though you chose (A) the first time around, God is such a good and loving God that He gives everyone a second chance to get it right. Look at the open book test (I am telling you the correct answer) he gave the Children of Israel.

Here is the test question (worth 100 points): If God gives you the choice to have (A), Life and blessings or (B), Death and curses, which of the two do you think is your better choice? The answer is found in *Deuteronomy 30:19*. This is an open book test. [Hint: the answer is (A)]

Deuteronomy 30:19 I call heaven and earth to record this day against you, that I have set before you life and death, blessing and cursing: therefore choose life, that both thou and thy seed may live:

Now 83 percent (10 out of 12) of these L.D., A.D.D., grown folks of Israel, flunked this easy open book test with its answer highlighted in bright yellow. They chose death rather than life in spite of being told the right answer. Can you believe that? Because they chose death and curses, they died in the wilderness and never entered the Promised Land. Even Moses failed this test and did not enter the Promised Land.

God gave Adam unprecedented freedom to eat of any tree in the garden and to name all the animals whatever he wanted to name them. He only gave Adam one restriction, one commandment, and one law. In *Genesis Chapter 3*, we will see that Adam could not keep that one commandment. If he could not keep just one commandment, how was he ever going to keep ten or more?

Here Comes the Bride

Genesis 2:18 And the LORD God said, It is not good that the man should be alone; I will make him an help meet for him.

Genesis 2:21 And the LORD God caused a deep sleep to fall upon Adam, and he slept: and he took one of his ribs, and closed up the flesh instead thereof;

Genesis 2:22 And the rib, which the LORD God had taken from man, made he a woman, and brought her unto the man.

Genesis 2:23 And Adam said, This is now bone of my bones, and flesh of my flesh: she shall be called Woman, because she was taken out of Man.

Genesis 2:24 Therefore shall a man leave his father and his mother, and shall cleave unto his wife: and they shall be one flesh.

Among the animal species, God created suitable mates (male and female) to accommodate the social and sexual needs of each species. However, Adam was alone. There was no one on earth who was compatible with him. There were no other human that he could have meaningful conversation and dialogue with, and there was no one like him to engage in sex with and enjoy all the pleasures and amenities that life had to offer. (Yeah, I know he probably had a dog as his best friend, but God was not going to allow bestiality in the garden. Therefore, God had to do something about this situation before Adam went off the deep end.

God gave Adam anesthesia, to numb him, and then performed the first medical operation. God gave Adam a her-sterectomy. (I know that is not a word found in the dictionary but we live in the 21st century, and we have the liberty to make up new words as needed, so that is one of my made-up words.) Remember, I told you earlier that Eve was in Adam from the beginning. Well, it was now time for her to come out in the name of Jesus. God cut Adam open, took one of the ribs close to his heart, and from that rib, he made the first woman.

Now imagine how beautiful and mind-blowingly fine Eve had to have been. This was the first woman God ever made. You know He wanted her to be a masterpiece second-to-none.

When Adam awakened, and God presented her to Adam, the first words out of Adam's mouth were, *"Whoa man, Dude, this is totally awesome! Wow! Ooh wee!! Oh my God! I have never, ever, seen anything so breathtaking! I cannot believe my eyes! Oh my God! Can I please take her for a test ride and get to know her?"*

God said, "Adam, you are tripping. Go ahead and do yo thang. Um out of here!"

Adam was so captivated and blown away that he lost focus of his responsibility as keeper of the garden and what God had said, concerning the Tree of Knowledge of Good and Evil, was the farthest thing from his mind. How could he think about the Law of God, with Eve flaunting all her luscious and voluptuous fruits of Eve-vil in his face 24/7/365? After seeing Eve and tasting the marvelous fruit of her lip-smacking, mouth-watering body, it would be a good while before Adam returned to thinking with his upper head.

Meanwhile, the devil knew he had only a limited window of opportunity before Adam regained his focus and sanity. He saw that Adam was crazy in love and had lost his mind drooling over Eve's incredible anatomy. This was the devil's prime opportunity to use Eve to deliver a fatal blow to Adam. In this defining moment, Eve had maximum influence over Adam. Therefore, the devil had to strike quickly while Eve had Adam's full and undivided attention, (if you know what I mean).

Genesis 2:25 *And they were both naked, the man and his wife, and were not ashamed.*

This point is important to note because all this was about to change forever. Adam and Eve were both butt naked, but there was no shame in it. They were like two innocent children running around in the nude with no indication that anything might be wrong. But for all practical purposes, they were also the only two humans on earth, so it was the same as a husband and wife with no children or other occupants, walking naked in the privacy of their home.

CHAPTER FIVE
The Birth of Evil
Misinformation Causes You To Miss Out

Knowledge Is Objective but Understanding Is Subjective

Now we turn the page to *Genesis Chapter Three. In Verse 1*, Satan arrives on the scene and immediately strikes up a conversation with Eve. The first thing to think of here is, why did Satan approach the woman rather than the man? To answer that question, we need to understand the difference between how men and women process information.

There is often conflict between men and women. They tend to frequently argue about various issues. But what is the number one reason why they have such conflict? Is it money? Is it sex? Is it religion? Is it cultural? Is it cheating? Is it the devil? All of these things may become the object of a given argument, but do any of them qualify as the number one reason why men and women have conflict?

Most conflicts between a man and his woman are because they are missing two critical things— information and understanding. Because they are missing these two things, they end up with misinformation and misunderstanding, which is WHY they have CONFLICT. If they had the right information and the right understanding of their information, they would know how to avoid or resolve the conflict.

Going back to what I explained in *Chapter 3* of this book, about Adam originally being a bi-gender being, he had male and female qualities. The male qualities reflected his masculinity, and the female qualities reflected his feminine qualities. The male component of man represents the intellect. The intellect is the thinking and information processing function of a man. The mind processes information, which is knowledge, and knowledge is objective. Objective means that *"It is what it is". It is neutral, unbiased, and impartial*. However, you can still have information (knowledge) and not have the right understanding of that knowledge.

Understanding is subjective and is representative of the female or subjective component of man. Subjective means that *there is a personal bias and is influenced by personal feelings, preferences, and opinions.* Your understanding of knowledge is subject to many factors such as what you believe, your education, your culture, your viewpoint, how you define key words, your feelings, motivation, objectives, and many other factors.

Factual information is objective, but understanding factual information is subjective. In other words, Truth is Truth, and what you think, feel, or believe, does not change the Truth. Even if you misinterpret or misunderstand the Truth, the Truth will still be the Truth. Your misunderstanding of the Truth just means that you don't really have the Truth. You just have your own version of something you believe to be true, but it is not the Truth. What you say and mean and what others understand you to say and mean, may not always be the same. This is why different people will have a different understanding of the same information.

A prime example is the Bible. Numerous people can have the same exact version of the Bible. In spite of them all having the same exact information, there is a broad spectrum of interpretations of that same information. That is why we have so many religions, denominations, different doctrines, conflicts, and confusion in the world today.

Therefore, when Satan has a choice of approaching a man or his woman with the intent to deceive, typically, he prefers approaching the woman. He understands that the man is more inclined to engage him intellectually, while the woman is more inclined to engage him emotionally. He also understands that if he can bypass your intellect and engage your emotions, he has a much greater chance of deceiving you.

He is more interested in challenging your understanding of the knowledge you have, rather than the knowledge itself. You can have the right information, but the wrong interpretation and understanding of that information. Satan is most successful when he is dealing with a person who has wrong information, wrong interpretation, and wrong understanding. Nevertheless, having the right information with wrong interpretation and wrong understanding works just as well for him.

Emotions Put Things in Motion
The devil approached Eve because he knew he could appeal to her emotions. Emotions actually play a vital active role in getting people to

act. You may give people the right information, but if they are not motivated to act on it, they will just store it as knowledge and do nothing with it. Think about all the books, educational materials, and seminars you have digested but have not put into practice. That is why if you only want to sit, share, and debate ideas and information, get a group of men together. However, if you really want to get the ball moving and get the job done, get a group of women together.

Women are typically more motivated to get things done because they are emotionally driven and they desire a host of things. Men primarily want sex, peace of mind, and the essential necessities of life. Men are motivated to want more, when their motivation is meeting the desires and needs of their wives and children. In general, a woman will do whatever it takes; to get the things she and her children need and want.

What Are Emotions?

Emotions are, *unreliable psychological expressions and reactions*. Emotional expressions include things like love, hate, anger, happiness, sadness, excitement, joy, passion, etc. These emotions cause people to act. They often trigger actions and behavior. If you look at the root word of *"emotion"*, it is *"motion"*. *Motion is the action or process of moving or being moved*. Emotions are thus related to your feelings and your passions.

However, emotions are mindless. Emotions do not think; they cause you to act. Intellect does not act. It thinks, evaluates, makes decisions, and directs. You may intellectually know you need or should do a certain thing at a certain time, but if you are angry, afraid, or unhappy about something, you are more than likely to do what you feel, rather than what you know is right or best to do.

Therefore, because the devil wanted to make something specific happen, he went to the woman. He elected not to go to the man because he did not want someone who was just going to hear what he had to say, think about it, and then do nothing or debate with him. He knew that the woman would listen to him if he approached her the right way and appealed to her emotions. He knew that if he was successful in convincing the woman, she was going to make it happen immediately. He knew that the woman had the power to persuade her husband to get with the program and do what the devil wanted.

The Serpent in Genesis 3 Was A Metaphor, Not A Literal Snake

The Bible depicts Satan as a serpent because a serpent is a very smooth and cunning creature. The devil is very crafty and knows how to smooth talk you into believing his lies.

Some people think that the devil appeared to Eve in the form of a literal snake. If that were so, it would mean that Adam saw him and heard him talking to Eve. The Bible states that Adam was with Eve when the encounter with the serpent took place.

If it were an actual serpent or snake, Adam would not have stood there allowing this conversation to ensue without taking any part in it. If it were an actual snake, and if Adam was any kind of man, he would have addressed the snake and said, *"Hold on Mr. Serpent, I am the man and keeper of this garden and that is my woman you are talking to. If you have something to say, you need to say it to me because I run things around here."*

Therefore, the serpent was a metaphoric and symbolic representation of the spirit of Satan. Eve was dealing with the same spirit we deal with on a daily basis. The spirit of Satan is what approaches our mind and proposes contrary ideas and suggestions for us to engage.

Although Adam was there with Eve, he could not see or hear what the devil was saying to her. It was a conversation going on in Eve's mind. Adam was not a mind reader and had no way of knowing what was going on in Eve's mind until she opened her mouth and shared her thoughts with Adam.

Once she told Adam what she was thinking, Adam had to decide whether he was going to buy into the lie. Adam knew what God had told him and now he was being presented with contrary information. Adam accepted this new information willfully and without questioning it. He was so fascinated and mesmerized by Eve that he mindlessly accepted what she presented to him.

This is no different from a man today who has an awesome looking woman who is rocking his world. He will do all sorts of things he would not normally do and take potentially devastating risks that he would not otherwise take to please her, keep her happy, and continue enjoying the pleasures of her delightful offerings. We have seen numerous men risk everything to please a woman and to get what he wants from her.

When a man loses his mind over a woman and becomes what is called "crazy in love", he becomes extremely vulnerable, especially if the woman is devious, unscrupulous, and easily deceived. Men should love their women and treat them like queens, but men should also guard their affections and think with their upper head.

What Makes a Woman More Susceptible?
A woman is an easier prey for the devil because; she is an emotionally driven creature whereas a man is an intellectually driven creature. The tendency of men is to approach a situation objectively by thinking and evaluating the facts, whereas women subjectively process information and situations, sensually and emotionally. It is all about their different feelings and perceptions of things. A woman is prone to falling prey, to things that make her feel good. When she sees something she wants intensely, she often will do whatever she needs to do to get it, especially if she is an ambitious and aggressive woman.

When the woman examined the Tree of Knowledge of Good and Evil, she saw that the tree was *good for food* (it was desirable to consume, it was useful, and thus of value), it was *pleasant to the eyes* (visually appealing), and, perceived as something that could *make her wise* (something to advance her intellectually, and thus enhance her social/economic status). This tree met all three conditions that motivate a woman to act. Notice that her motivation to buy into Satan's lie had nothing to do with sex. It had every thing to do with her values, sensory nature, feelings, and self-image.

This is why a man, will wine and dine a woman, take her to nice places, and buy her nice things. These things make her feel good, special, and appreciated. This is why you see some of the most beautiful and finest women in the world with some of the ugliest and dorkiest men. Money can buy most of the things women desire, and these things make them feel a certain way, the way they want to feel. Perhaps, this is why they are called (fee-males and not free-males). It will cost a man a lot to have and keep his woman. He will pay that price in various ways. Men who are poor or can barely provide for themselves, ought to seriously consider this fact when contemplating marriage.

Women want the things that make them feel and look good, and men want to get laid. Men will do what they need to do to get laid, and women will do whatever they need to do to get paid for being laid. When I say get paid, I am not just referring to money, but anything a woman wants. A man has to give her what she wants if he wants to get what he is after. In a nutshell, that is the way it is with humans.

The Secret To Getting What You Want

Men are very simple creatures. They have one switch that turns them on and off. That switch is their sex drive. If his woman is giving him good sex, he is turned on and happy as a pig in a grocery store. If she is denying him sex, or the sex is not good to him, he is turned off and will seek pleasure elsewhere. It is that simple.

However, the key to a good relationship is for both parties to do right by the other. Each partner should always give what is rightfully due to the other. If both parties are giving what is due, both will be receiving what they want and need, thus eliminating dissatisfaction and the temptation to go elsewhere.

Women, on the other hand, are complex illogical beings. They are definitely from Venus, but that is okay. Many things turn a woman on and off. She has various physical, material, emotional, and psychological, wants and needs. If a man wants his woman to keep him turned on, he must study his woman and learn how to satisfy and tweak all her various needs and wants.

It is kind of like a combination lock on a safe. You have to dial the right combination for the lock to open. If a man does not study his woman, he will not know the right sequence of numbers and will remain locked out. However, if he is not careful, another man will study her also and figure out the right code, and the next thing he will know is, the other man has taken his wife away. (Sometimes that can be a blessing in disguise).

Men have a hard time understanding how to keep their women happy. They try to deal logically with their women. What they do not understand is that a woman is an emotionally driven creature, and emotions are not subject to logic. Therefore, insisting on dealing with your woman logically, is actually, illogical. God made man the leader, so he must be the first to demonstrate true love and respect, so his woman will have a clear model to follow. Nevertheless, he must also learn to know and understand his woman if he wants to maintain peace and get a piece whenever he wants it.

It is natural for a woman to respond emotionally and psychologically to stimuli. Doing so does not make her a bad woman; it is actually part of what makes her a woman. God designed her this way to make a man love and appreciate her. Otherwise, a man would just treat her as a sex object and dog her out after he gets what he wants. God forbid! It is about loving her, not barking out commands and orders. That is dictatorship! God intended the marriage relationship to be romantic and stimulating, rather than mechanical and dutiful.

Wait a minute, ladies, just because your man has not learned the art of romance yet, does not mean that you should sell your body to the highest bidder. Again, God forbid! Many men do not know how to be romantic. A woman teaches a man how to treat her from the onset of the relationship. The real problem is when a woman sells herself cheap at the beginning of a relationship. Women give up the sex before marriage and when or if they finally do get married, the thrill is just about gone. The woman often allows the man to practice "wham bam, thank you mam" before marriage and by the time they get married, he has become a pro at short-changing her and she has gotten use to it.

Furthermore, romance without finance, can often become a nuisance to the relationship. Women enjoy a man wining and dining them, and they most certainly enjoy gifts and surprises. They get very annoyed with hearing repeatedly, "we can't afford it". (Remember, they are fee-males not free- males) Men, treat your woman like a queen and honor her. Ladies, treat your man like a king, and give him due respect, plenty of good sex, love, and lots of ego stroking.

Men and Women Are Designed to Complement Each Other

The relationship between a man and woman is like the relationship between the mind and the body. The body is equipped with sensorial capabilities that enable humans to see, smell, taste, feel, and hear. God endowed women with an intensified ability to sense certain things more than a man does. They are more sensitive to emotional and sensual stimuli. They often notice and key in on things that men are totally oblivious to seeing or understanding.

The body senses things and communicates that information back to the brain. The brain in turn, processes the information and decides what to do with it. This is how God created a man and a woman to function in harmony with each other. Each was endowed with a primary function that they do best. When they allow each other to do what they do best, they end up with good results in a marriage.

The perfect example is how God designed the man to produce human seeds called sperms. He equipped the woman with the ability to receive the seed from a man and have it grow and develop into a human being within her body. A man cannot impregnate himself or another man, and he cannot produce a baby. A woman cannot impregnate herself, another woman, or a man. This unique design causes the man and the woman to need each other for reproduction. God also gave other unique abilities and functions to men and women that require them to need each other to accomplish certain things.

Woman: The Man's Kryptonite

Kryptonite is the substance that made Superman weak. A man's kryptonite is a woman. A woman is capable of destroying the most powerful of men. A single woman stripped Sampson, who could defeat a thousand men with the jawbone of an ass, of his mighty power. Satan knew that he had a much greater chance to defeat Adam by using Eve than by confronting Adam head on. He knew if he approached Adam first, Adam would have likely grabbed his Bible and Strong's Concordance and start quoting Scriptures and having theological debates with him. Eve on the other hand, would become caught up in the smoothness of Satan's voice and how what the devil was saying was making her feel.

What is so peculiar about a woman is that she fear lizards, rats, and roaches, but she will rear up at a man in a heartbeat, (especially a black woman). She will boldly challenge a man, but if a rodent confronts her, she become hysterically fearful and calls her man to fight her battle against that little tiny mouse or rat. (Go figure! Shaking My Head SMH) I have seen a single roach run a woman out of her house in the middle of the night, and she would not return until she found a man to come kill the roach. (SMH)

The devil is fully aware of a woman's seductive power over a man. He understands that it is easier to deceive a woman quicker than a man because a woman often emotionally and sensually processes information. Therefore, his strategy is to use his craftiness to deceive the woman, and the woman would then use her seductive power to bring down the man. (An awesome strategy)

A beautiful and curvaceous woman is obviously tempting, attractive, sexy, enticing, alluring, irresistible, provocative, and flirtatious. Her anatomy is endowed with sensual and sexually appealing parts. She is alluringly attractive and appealing from her eyes to her thighs, from her nose to her toes, and from her lips to her hips, and every point in between.

A woman of such fine caliber can make a man do senseless things. She can make a man say, *"If loving you is wrong, I don't want to do right. If being without you means doing right, then I'd rather be wrong than right."* This is precisely the effect Eve had on Adam. Adam was so dumbfounded by her breathtaking beauty that, he forgot who he was and who he was supposed to be.

How the Devil Deceived Eve?

The devil deceived Eve by engaging her in an intellectual head conversation. Satan spoke to her mind by communicating suggestive thoughts. His objective was first to find out if Eve had received the correct information from God. Secondly, he wanted to learn about her understanding of the information. By engaging Eve in an exploratory conversation, Satan was able to determine where she was in terms of her knowledge and understanding. Whenever Satan encounters a believer who has very limited and erroneous information and lacks understanding, he knows he has hit the jackpot.

An uneducated believer is the devil's best customer. Deceiving an ignorant believer is like taking candy from a newborn baby. If Satan makes his lie sound true enough, the uninformed believer will believe just about anything the devil says. So let us examine the conversation between Eve and Satan.

Genesis 3:1 Now the serpent was more subtil than any beast of the field which the LORD God had made. And he said unto the woman, Yea, hath God said, Ye shall not eat of every tree of the garden?

Genesis 3:2 And the woman said unto the serpent, We may eat of the fruit of the trees of the garden:

Genesis 3:3 But of the fruit of the tree which is in the midst of the garden, God hath said, Ye shall not eat of it, neither shall ye touch it, lest ye die.

Genesis 3:4 And the serpent said unto the woman, Ye shall not surely die:

Genesis 3:5 For God doth know that in the day ye eat thereof, then your eyes shall be opened, and ye shall be as gods, knowing good and evil.

In this conversation, Satan asked Eve a probing question.
He asks Eve, *"Did God say you could not eat of any of the trees?*
Eve replied, *"No, that's not what he said. God said we may eat of the fruit of the trees of the garden: But of the fruit of the tree which is in the midst of the garden, God hath said, Ye shall not eat of it, neither shall ye touch it, lest ye die."*

Now let's go back and see what God actually said to Adam and whether or not Eve got it right in her conversation with Satan.

Genesis 2:9 *And out of the ground made the LORD God to grow every tree that is pleasant to the sight, and good for food; the tree of life also in the midst of the garden, and the tree of knowledge of good and evil.*

Genesis 2:16 *And the LORD God commanded the man, saying, Of every tree of the garden thou mayest freely eat:*

Genesis 2:17 *But of the tree of the knowledge of good and evil, thou shalt not eat of it: for in the day that thou eatest thereof thou shalt surely die.*

When You Don't Know Exactly What God Said, You Are Likely to Believe Anything That Sounds Good

The first big mistake Eve made was that she indicated that, *God forbade them to eat of the tree in the midst of the garden.* The problem with that reply was, there were two trees in the midst of the garden. God had specified exactly which of the two trees was forbidden. Eve did not specify which one in her conversation with Satan. Therefore, she may not have been sure which tree was the forbidden tree.

She therefore went ahead and injected her own addendum to what God had said.

Eve casually added, *"Neither shall you touch it".*

God never said that part. Adding to or taking away from what was originally said can sometimes change the whole meaning. I am not referring here to translating, paraphrasing, or adding clarity or insight to Scriptures. I am talking about whenever Scriptures are purposely or ignorantly altered to distort, pervert, or change their meaning or intent. (God promises a curse upon whosoever does that).

Eve was revealing to Satan, precisely what he wanted to know, which was, that Eve did not really know the Scripture. She did not really know what God said. So Satan knew that, since she was not clear on what God really said, he could refute what God said and then offer her a compelling reason why God had lied to them both. That would make her feel like God lied to conceal the truth, to keep them ignorant of who they were, and keep them from being gods themselves.

Satan emphatically told Eve, *"You shall not surely die!"* Satan was telling Eve without actually saying it, that God was a no-good liar. Satan indicated that God was trying to keep Adam and Eve blind to who they were and God did not want them to know the difference between good and evil. Satan told her that *as soon as she ate of the tree, her eyes would be opened, and she would know that she was a god.* She would know both good and evil. Now, parts of what Satan said were true, but other parts were not totally true.

When Satan said, *"You shall not surely die"* that was a lie. However, from the perspective of Adam and Eve physically dying immediately, that was true. They were not immediately going to die physically. The word "die" means *to become mortal*, which means *certain to die eventually*. Adam and Eve initially, were immortal beings, possessing eternal life as long as they did not eat of the only tree that was poisonous and would cause them to experience mortality. After they sinned, they became both *mortal* and *immoral* beings. They did however, immediately die spiritually. The Tree of Life gave Adam and Eve eternal life and made them immortal. Conversely, disobeying God by eating of the Tree of Knowledge is what produced or caused death to come upon them and downgraded them to mere mortals.

Then the devil said to her, *her eyes would be opened*. That was true. Moreover, *they will be as gods knowing good and evil*, and that was true. Looking at the parts that were true and looking at the part that was not true, it looks like most of what Satan said was true. The problem was that the part that was not true had the greatest consequence. The part of becoming mortal beings (dying spiritually first, physically secondly, and eternally thirdly) is the most damning part of the whole issue.

Living in Paradise, having it "made in the shade", not having to get up every day, not having to drive in rush hour traffic, and not having to go to work is priceless. Having to give that up to go live in the Hood and go to work making chump change and deal with a host of other hassles and issues is next to living in Hell by comparison. Adam and Eve believed something that had a certain amount of truth to it, but the part that was a lie was what caused them to suffer great loss and experience major consequences.

This of course is how the devil works. He will inject a bit of truth into his lie, so the part that is true, is what gets you to accept the part that is a lie. If 3 out of 4 things said sound true or are true, you may have the tendency to believe that everything about it is true. That is what deception is about. It is like counterfeit currency where most of the bill looks authentic, but there is one little something missing or one little something that is not right, which disqualifies the whole bill from being authentic.

Don't Let Satan Edit Your Mindset

Your mindset is your personal way of thinking and believing. It consists of the information, principles, and beliefs you have adopted and registered as the way you process information and make decisions. Once you set your mind, that program is saved and will become the basis of all of your decision-making.

If you have filled your mind with righteous principles, the devil will of course seek to hack your mind and attempt to edit your program. He hacks your mind by engaging you in head conversations. He will suggest alternative viewpoints and suggest that you edit your mindset. If you change your mindset to include his suggestions and decide to act on his suggestions, you will produce an error message, which is sin. This is what happened to Eve.

God Protects Those He Loves That Belong to Him

God protects his own from hurt, harm, and danger. It is no different from earthly parents who truly love and care for their children. An earthly parent recognizes that a child is limited in knowledge about certain things that can be harmful. The parent therefore, does whatever is necessary to keep the child safe, and educate the child, so the child can eventually be knowledgeable and mature enough to make responsible decisions alone. This is precisely how God deals with his spiritual children. Our Heavenly Father knows best, because He knows, sees, and hears everything.

A mother when she is busy doing other things may put her baby in a playpen to restrict him from getting into trouble and bringing harm to himself. She limits the child access to the surrounding environment, because the child does not know that certain things outside the playpen, can be harmful, because he does not know yet, how to responsibly use or interact with them.

A mother will instruct a child, not to play with the electrical outlet or touch the hot stove. Now if the child has never experienced an electrical shock or a burn from a hot stove, he has no idea of what to expect. Nevertheless, he is curious by nature, and wants to know, why his loving mother is keeping him from experiencing something that looks interesting, and will increase his knowledge of his environment.

In the mind of the child, Momma is denying him the right to satisfy his natural curiosity. The child says to himself, *"As soon as she leaves the room, I will quickly go explore these forbidden territories and then return to the place where she left me".* However, when doing that, something goes terribly wrong with his plan.

After the child touches the hot stove, he experiences a severe burning sensation, and it causes him to scream and cry loudly. His mom comes running, yelling, *"Didn't I tell you not to touch that (#%&*) hot stove"!* Then the child thinks, *"How the heck did she know, that is what I did? She must have the gift of knowledge."* (Duh!)

This is what happened to Adam and Eve. They let their curiosity cause them to experiment with what God forbade. As a result, God evicted them both from the Garden of Eden and forced them to work hard for a living and be subject to a host of adversities and undesirable issues in life.

God wants us to trust him, and trust whatever He tells us because, He knows what He is talking about. On the other hand, we are like infants. We do not know much about many things, in both the visible, and the invisible world. Consequently, we are likely to make many bad, even harmful, decisions if we rely on our own very limited knowledge and understanding.

Nevertheless, God as a loving Father has provided us with information useful to guide our lives and keep us on the path of righteousness. If we consistently listen to what He advises and do what He tells us to do, we will be safe from harm and will prosper in all our ways.

Adam Did Not Do His Job
Genesis 3:6 And when the woman saw that the tree was good for food, and that it was pleasant to the eyes, and a tree to be desired to make one wise, she took of the fruit thereof, and did eat, and <u>gave also unto her husband with her</u>; and <u>he did eat</u>.

Eve saw that the tree was very appealing and offered several desirable benefits. This is another key part of the devil's strategy. When he offers you something that God forbids or opposes, he will make it appealing to your flesh, to your eyes, and to your ego. He will sell you on all the benefits: How it will make you feel, look, be seen by others; how it will make you rich, famous, popular, etc. He will not show you what his offer is going to do to you in the end. He is not going to show you what you are forfeiting. All he wants is, for you to reject God's offer and ways, and accept, his ways. He wants you to forfeit eternal life, so you can spend eternity tormented with him. Misery loves company.

When Eve ventured out to explore the Tree of Knowledge of Good and Evil, she was just doing, what a woman was designed to do. She was checking things out. She went shopping. Eve brought her newly discovered information back to Adam, just as she was supposed to do. She did not hide it from him. She shared it with him.

The real problem was with Adam. Adam was supposed to examine the information to determine if it was in harmony and alignment with the Word of God. Adam did not do his job. Instead, he just accepted what Eve presented to him without evaluating it and blindly stamped his seal of approval on it. Eve drank the Kool-Aid and gave it to Adam, who was right there with her when all of this went down, and he drank the Kool-Aid also.

Adam's responsibility was to keep the garden. That meant he had to make sure that everybody and everything remained in alignment with the Will of God and in compliance with His Law. Adam was the sheriff. His duty was to uphold and enforce the Law of God, not break it.

So we see "the sheriff" instead of arresting the transgressor, getting spiritually into bed with the transgressor and becoming a transgressor. When the sheriff becomes the criminal, he disqualifies himself to serve as sheriff, and that relegates him to the status of a criminal, and thus subject to receiving the same punishment and fate assigned to a criminal. This is what happened to Adam. He disqualified himself to rule as God on earth and became instead a wretched sinner and a lawbreaker.

Why Did Adam Transgress The Law?
1Timothy 2:14 And Adam was not deceived, but the woman being deceived was in the transgression.

Adam was not deceived, but his wife who was deceived influenced him. If Adam was not deceived, then why would he let his wife convince him to forfeit the Kingdom of God, his right to rule as God, his gated community, and all the amenities and perks of being King over the earth? The answer is quite simple. It was sex. That is right! The almighty vagina!

Before Eve came on the scene, Adam did not know what death was, and he had never experienced sex with a woman. He was a virgin. After he experienced sex with Eve, he still had no knowledge of death. At that point, Adam knew what it was like not to have a woman and not to have sex. He had come to know how wonderful having sex was.

Then when Eve offered Adam to eat from the forbidden tree, Adam's mind was not on God, it was on Eve and on sex. Furthermore, Adam was not going back to not having sex. In his mind, that was simply not an option. Adam's mindset was, once you get cat, you can't go back! It's like going black or going Mac. Once you go black or Mac, you don't go back. It's like that!

Now picture this scene. As a man, God blessed you with the most beautiful and finest woman on the planet earth. She has captivated your full attention. You are beholding the awesomeness of her total anatomical design and attentively exploring all the wondrous features thereof.

Now tell me, (A) Would your mind be focused on some rule God gave you about not eating of a particular tree, or (B) Would your mind be focused on the luscious fruits hanging off the body of your voluptuous woman and the joy and pleasure they all offer you?

If you answered (A), you are likely a liar and the truth is not in you, or you are seriously gay. But if you answered (B), you are keeping it real and have just passed the test for being a legitimate man.

Adam saw that nothing strange had happen to Eve yet and perhaps what she was saying had some truth and validity to it. After all, the devil said, *"You shall not surely die."* Adam did not see anything different or weird happening to Eve, so he apparently figured, that there was nothing much to this dying thing, and maybe it was true, that they would not die just as Satan had told Eve.

I Can See

When Eve ate of the forbidden tree, nothing happened. As soon as Adam ate of the tree, their eyes were opened, and they did know good and evil, and Adam exclaimed, *"Oh my God! I can see! I can see! Oh my God, we are butt naked!"*

Nothing happened until after Adam had sinned. God gave the commandment to Adam and held him personally responsible for keeping it. It was his responsibility to bring his wife back into compliance with God's ordinance. Even today, a man still has the responsibility to rule his home. If his wife or his children step out of alignment, it is the man's responsibility to bring them back into alignment. If they rebel against him and refuse to correct the error of their ways, just as God personally chastised Miriam, Moses' sister, for murmuring against Moses, God will do likewise, to whosoever refuses to submit to the authority that He has ordained.

This new experience of seeing themselves as naked, left them both feeling shameful and embarrassed. Adam was not sure if this shameful feeling had anything to do with death, but he knew it was an uncomfortable feeling. They began to relate the feeling they had before eating of the forbidden tree to what was considered 'good' and realizing that what they were feeling after eating of the tree must be 'evil'. Their shameful feeling changed everything. They suddenly felt they needed to cover up their nakedness.

The opening of their eyes meant that *they became consciously aware of good and evil*. Whereas before, they were like little children, they did not know the difference. They had never before experienced evil. Now that they had become aware of their wrongdoing, they attempted to remedy the situation by sewing fig leaves to make aprons to cover their nakedness. (I am not sure where they found a needle and thread so quickly, considering it had not been invented yet.) (LOL)

They went from not knowing the difference between good and evil to becoming wanna-be tailors. The clothes they made were jacked-up, and God later had to make them decent looking outfits to wear. Trying to cover up their sin by making clothes, could not take away the guilty feelings they were experiencing in their hearts and conscience.

What Is Nakedness?

Naked, in one sense, means that *they were uncovered, exposed, and vulnerable*, and it also means *they had nothing to hide or be ashamed of*. All before while Adam and Eve were naked, they felt neither shame nor a need to hide or cover their nakedness. As soon as they both had sinned, they became aware of their nakedness both physically and spiritually. Although they could physically see they were naked all the while, they did not know that they were naked versus being clothed. Being naked was all they ever knew. Therefore, in their minds, it was normal and natural. However, when they had sinned, the eyes of their understanding were opened. All of a sudden, they had a eureka moment. They had a revelation. They were naked, and naked all of a sudden became something bad.

I suspect they first understood that they were spiritually naked. That feeling of shame made them realize something had dramatically changed. They did not know how to cover their spiritual nakedness, so they resorted to covering their physical nudity. When humans sin, their first attempt is to try to cover or mask their sin.

For example, if a man cheats on his wife, he tries to hide his cheating from his wife. If she becomes suspicious or finds a piece of evidence that indicates he may be cheating, he will begin to make excuses or fabricate lies and deceptions to try to conceal his sin. Instead of confessing his sin and asking for forgiveness, he does everything in his power to hide the truth from his wife. When she finally catches him red-handed, it is then, and only then that he decides to admit his guilt. Women cheat also and do the same thing. I just used the man as an example.

When Adam heard God approaching him, his first reaction was to try to hide from God, which showed his true ignorance. How can you hide from God or hide something from God? That is impossible. Nevertheless, Adam tried to hide from God. He was really showing off his ignorance. If we rewind this video and replay it from the beginning, we will see the steps involved when we try to conceal sin. First Adam realized he did wrong, then he started feeling shameful, next he tried to cover up his fault, then he tried to hide from God, then God busted him, and then he started blaming Eve and God for his own moral failure.

Adam said to God, *"The woman you gave me is responsible for my disobedience. She caused me to sin against you. It's not my fault"*. He was thus telling God that his sin was primarily God's fault. He was insinuating that if God had left him single and alone, and had not bought this sinful woman into his life, he would have never sinned. Therefore, it was God's fault and the woman's fault.

Adam refused to take personal responsibility for his own actions. Perhaps, if Adam had admitted his wrongness and asked for forgiveness, God would have given him a slap on the hand, kicked them both out of the garden, and given him an easy county job where he would not have had to work so hard. But no! Adam wanted to act as if he was the innocent victim of God and also a victim of Eve. In his mind, it was not his fault that he broke the law; it was God's and Eve's fault.

When we try to cover our sins or deny that we have sinned, our sin will keep us at odds with God. *But if we confess our sins, God is faithful and just and will forgive us and cleanse us from all unrighteousness*. Therefore, if

Adam and Eve had come to God correctly, God would have forgiven Adam and Eve and put them back in good standing with Him.

1 John 1:8 *If we say that we have no sin, we deceive ourselves, and the truth is not in us.*

1 John 1:9 *If we confess our sins, he is faithful and just to forgive us our sins, and to cleanse us from all unrighteousness.*

God Be Cool

When Adam sinned and God saw it, He blew his stack.

The Father said to the Son, *"Do you see what that idiot just did? I can't believe he is that stupid? I gave him one simple commandment and he could not keep it! He has thousands of trees to eat from, but no, he had to eat from the very tree I commanded him not to eat from. But what really ticks me off is that they believed the devil over me. Can you believe that?"*

The Son (Jesus) then said, *"I feel you, but Father, you really need to calm down. I understand your frustration. Just wait until later when everything cools down and you have had a chance to think about it before you act."* The Son then said, *"Remember also what your Word says, be quick to listen, slow to speak and slow to anger".* **(James 1:19)**

God replied, Yeah, you're right.

So, God waited until He had finished blowing off steam and had cooled down. In the cool of the day, God finally confronted Adam. They both heard God coming and they tried to hide themselves among the trees.

God called out, *"Adam, where are you?"*

Adam replied, *"Um over here hiding from you, because I found out, I am naked".*

Then God said, *"You fool, you have been naked all the while".*

Adam replied, *"Yeah, but I did not know that before my eyes were opened".*

Then God asked, *"What's up with that. Who told you, that you were naked"*

Adam's Conscience Told Him That He Was Naked

The human conscience is an inner feeling or voice that acts as a guide to note the rightness or wrongness of our behavior. Your conscience will accuse you or excuse you. When we do something wrong, our conscience lets us know we have done wrong, by either making us feel guilty and bad, or by accusing us. A typical conversation may go something like this after we do something wrong:

Your conscience confronts you by saying, *"You know that was dead wrong what you just did."*

You respond to your conscience by saying, *"What are you talking about?"*

Your conscience then says, *"Don't play dumb. You know exactly what I am talking about. You know what you just did."*

You try to explain. *"Oh that? Well. I didn't mean to do that".* (This is known as lying to yourself)

Your conscience rebukes you and says, *"Stop lying, you know you intentionally did it. You need to repent and ask God for forgiveness."*

Then you say, *"I'm going to keep this to myself, and I swear I won't do it again".*

Your conscience replies, saying, *"Whatever dude. You need to listen to me. I am here to help you stay in good standing with God. If you don't listen to me, I can't help you. You are defeating my whole purpose."*

All too often, people override their consciences. They justify their wrongdoing in their minds and ignore the 'little voice' inside their heads. When you treat your conscience in this way, your conscience stop bothering you and lets you do whatever you want to do. However, later, when you begin to suffer the consequences of what you did wrong, your conscience speaks out again and says, *"I tried to tell you right, but you refused to listen to me. Stubborn idiot! This is what you get for not listening to me."*

Immediately after Adam ate of the forbidden tree, Adam and Eve's consciences spoke to them and said, *"Y'all, done messed up. You've sinned against God, and now you are going to die. That was plain stupid!"*

Then their conscience spoke up and said, *"You are naked, and from now on, you will be exposed to spiritual attacks and susceptible to evil".*

Adam then asked, *"What should we do?"*

His conscience responded and said, *Why are you asking me? You are not going to do what I tell you. Repent fool?*

Instead of listening and obeying his conscience, Adam leaned toward his own understanding once again. He decided to try to cover his nakedness, but in spite of doing that, he still felt guilty and ashamed.

Adam actually ignored God's question when God asked, *"Who told you that you were naked?* Adam never answered that question. Instead, Adam sidestepped the question and immediately started playing the blame game. Adam told God that *it was God's fault and also Eve's fault.* She was why he ate of the forbidden tree.

Adam offer God a lame excuse implying, *"That captivating woman you gave me, she gave me the fruit, and yeah, I ate it. What else was I going to do?"* Then Adam added, *"Man you don't understand, I couldn't tell that woman 'no'. She makes me do crazy things. I find myself doing whatever she wants."*

Then God turned to Eve and asked her, *"What is it you have done?"*
Eve replied, *"It's not my fault. The devil made me do it. We were just having a casual conversation and he started asking me questions and started insinuating that you lied to us. He convinced me that he was telling the truth."*

Eve continued and said more. *"His smooth talking and cool approach kind of threw me for a loop and I guess I was deceived. He was so convincing and he was also somewhat cute. Yeah, Adam was right there with me, and he did not say one word. He should have said something! He's supposed to be the man! He didn't handle his business, so why are you sweating me?"*

When humans sin, all too often they want to blame the devil or someone else for what they did wrong. We have a tendency to lie to ourselves, lie to, and on others, and refuse to take personal responsibility for our own sinful actions. This is why God said, *David was a man after his own heart*, not because David was so righteous, but because David was man enough to own up to his sin when his sin was discovered, instead of trying to deny it. God just wants us to keep it real and come correct, by confessing and forsaking our sins.

We Are Tempted By Our Own Lusts

The devil frequently introduces ungodly thoughts to our minds. Our job is to examine those thoughts, determine if they are in harmony and alignment with the Word and the Will of God. If a thought is not, we should reject the idea and mark it as evil. We are tempted when we entertain ungodly thoughts that appeal to our carnal nature. When such thoughts lure us away from rightness and cause us to partake of what is ungodly, we fall into sin. If we do not repent of that sin and forsake it, that sin will become a habitual practice. We will become carriers of an evil virus and producers of evil works.

People make a conscious choice to engage and practice ungodly behavior. Sin begins with a desire to experience a particular lust or forbidden thing. Once you taste and see that it feels good, you subsequently decide to continuously engage it. When the influence of that lust become addictive and dominates your thinking and decision-making ability, you become a slave to it. In order to regain control of your life and return to normalcy, you must make a conscious decision to divorce the lustful activity and return to doing what is right.

Quite often, people who are trapped in sin feel powerless to be free from it. They sometimes need others to help them regain control of their lives. Regardless of whether that help comes from a secular or a spiritual source, the objective is to help the person make a conscious decision to forsake the evil they are in bondage to and return to what is right.

God Is a Loving, Merciful, and Forgiving God
Some people think that Adam sinned because he wanted to stand by his woman. That is bull scripture! Adam knew that God was very capable of making him another woman as beautiful and as fine as Eve was. After all, Adam still had some spare ribs. If Adam had stayed faithful to God's command, God being the merciful, forgiving, and loving God that He is, would have allowed Adam to decide, what he wanted to do about Eve.

Adam was made in the image (character) of God. Therefore, he would have responded to Eve in the same manner, as God would have. Even if Adam had been too confused to decide, he would have asked God for advice. God says that *if any man lacks wisdom, let him ask God for it.* That is what Solomon did.

It is clear to me that God would have spared Eve and made a way for her to be reconciled to Him. This is exactly what He did for Adam and Eve anyway. They both sinned, and God did not visit immediate physical death upon them. After He told them what their punishment was, God immediately introduced His plan to save humanity through his Son. That plan would crush the head of the devil.

Lucifer was the first to sin against God and that is why he was kicked out of Heaven. However, God did not destroy him right away nor confine him to Hell. He expelled him from Heaven and cast him down to earth. When the Children of Israel sinned in the Promised Land, God punished them, but He also gave them an opportunity to redeem themselves.

When Moses came down from the mountain with the Ten Commandments, the Children of Israel were having a big block party to celebrate and worship their new golden calf idol god. Moses was so angry that he simultaneously broke all ten Commandments. God was so furious that He was about to seriously drop death on all of them.

Moses pleaded with God not to kill the people. That is what a true leader is supposed to do. He stands in the gap and begs for mercy for those he loves, and God usually responds favorably if they have not already pushed their luck to the limit. Adam would have most likely have taken this same course of action if he had not eaten from the forbidden tree.

It is the nature of God to use physical death lastly. The only time God drops the bomb on humans immediately is when He is making a statement, proving a point, or demonstrating that He ain't playing around. Other than that, God is normally merciful and liberally gives us grace. If God was not merciful and gracious, I would not be around to write this book, and you would not be around to read it. This same spirit of grace and mercy is what He would have put in Adam's heart toward Eve, if Eve, were the only one who sinned.

CHAPTER SIX
Woman:
The Most Powerful Creature on Earth

The Power of a Woman

A woman is the most powerful creature on earth. Throughout the history of humankind, women have managed to influence men's behavior and decisions. Beginning with Adam and Eve, Eve influenced and persuaded Adam to disobey God. Adam was given authority to rule the entire earth. God gave him complete control over everything, commanded him to not eat of the Tree of Knowledge of good and evil, and told Adam that if he did, he would surely die.

Adam was given all authority on earth backed by the full power and authority of God. Yet, he forfeited all that, at the simple request of his woman. She did not put a gun to his head, she did not issue terrorist threats, she did not bribe him with money or come with an army to force him to submit to her will. She just simply influenced him to partake in sin with her by persuading him to do what God had forbidden. Wow! That is some serious power. No guns, no bombs, no nothing... just a simple "Honey do this for me. Okay baby?" Adam did not argue or give any resistance. None!

Now which of Eve's power tools do you think she used to cause Adam to forfeit his authority over the entire earth? Considering that they both were already naked and Eve's body was masterfully sculpted, she no doubt commanded Adam's full and undivided attention in more ways than one. Eve had also determined she was not going down by herself. She made sure, that if she had to do "the time for the crime", she was going to have company. In that moment, Adam forgot all about what was at stake and that was his mistake.

Therefore, we see that in the very first story about a relationship between a man and his woman, the woman had extraordinary power to influence her man to forfeit his kingdom and be evicted from his paradise, his oasis. King Herod offered up to half of his kingdom to a young woman just to see her dance. Adam took that offer to a whole nother level, for he was willing to forfeit his whole kingdom, and he was even willing to die and go to Hell for Eve. Adam obviously was not thinking with the right head. (Lord, do grant me the strength to resist Eve-vil)

The Far Reaching Influence and Impact of Women

After considering the influence, impact, and value that women bring to the table of life, I have concluded that, women are the most powerful creatures on earth. Obviously, I am not speaking in terms of their physical power or strength. Of course, most men are physically stronger than most women, and certainly there are animals that are much more powerful than men, in terms of physical strength.

However, when you consider the power of influence and their world impact, I believe there is no more powerful creature than a woman. James Brown recorded a song called *"This Is A Man's World"*. In that song, his main point was that although this is a world physically and politically dominated by men, the world is meaningless and boring without the presence of the female species.

In reality, women secretly run and rule the world if the truth were actually told. Men are in the driver's seat, but women are the ones telling them where to go. It is exactly like riding in a taxicab. The cab driver is in the front seat behind the wheel, but the passenger in the back seat is directing the journey. Many men occupying high positions as world leaders are also highly influenced by their wives and/or mistresses.

To demonstrate the power of women, just imagine that all the women suddenly vanished from the world. Well, a great number of men would lose their minds. Some men are so dependent on their women that if they lose them, they would not know what to do. Some men are still momma's boys and can barely live without their mother.

If you suddenly took all the women out of the world, the world's economy would collapse. All shoe stores would immediately go out of business. Many grocery stores and shopping malls would fail and shut down. Strip clubs and nightclubs will most certainly go belly up. The absence of women would be more devastating than any natural disaster. It would be more crippling than a U.S. financial institution meltdown. The Great Depression would be a time of prosperity in comparison. Conversely, if all men were taken out of the social economic equation, women would simply pick up the pieces, make the necessary adjustments, and keep everything moving right along as it always has.

As far as sex is concerned, many women have already turned their affections toward one another and are deploying sexual toys to satisfy their sexual needs and urges. They have learned to pleasure themselves by any means necessary. Therefore, a man has become only one of many options available to a woman and not always the most desired option. The sex toy industry is a 15 billion dollar industry and 44 percent of women age 18 to 60 have used a sex toy.

Women make the world go around. Men would rather contend with a vicious invasion from alien forces than to have all women removed from the earth. If all the women were gone, men would just be sitting around playing golf, shooting pool, watching sports, and drinking beer. Oh yeah, I forgot, fishing. What else would there be for them to do? Jesus may as well come back immediately if that were to happen because we would have a situation worse than Sodom and Gomorrah. Men would inevitably turn to one another to fulfill their lustful and sexual appetites.

In addition to the economic impact, having no women would have on the world, over time, the population would also dwindle to nothing because there would be no women to produce babies. Eventually, animals would greatly outnumber people, and the animals would consume humankind and take over the world. Humans would become the hunted instead of the hunters. The animals would flip the script and become the hunters.

Women are the ones who give birth to children and usually the ones who raise the children and shape their morals, beliefs, and character. Women are the predominant ones who are teaching children in school. Both men and children greatly depend on women to do a lot for them. A woman's job is never done. Between home, work, church, and social life, she is always busy doing something for someone, and much of the time that 'something' is for a male person.

When you consider all these things as well as all the things I have not mentioned, it becomes very evident why I say that women are the most influential and impactful creatures on earth and hence, the most powerful creature on earth. That's because they are.

If you exiled all the women in America to another country and did not allow them to have any interactions or commerce with America, America would collapse or become a Third World country. No doubt, if all women were exiled from America, the church would also become extinct because it is predominately women who support and attend church.

If it were not for women, Jesus would have had to go looking for his disciples when he rose from the dead because his cowardly disciples most certainly did not come looking for him. It was the women who went down to the tomb early in the morning to check on Jesus, and after they discovered that He had risen from the dead, they went to deliver the good news to his fearful and faithless disciples. As far as those disciples were concerned, Jesus was dead like Moses was and gone forever.

Furthermore, if you banished all the women, the vast majority of children and pets would have to go with them because most men are not going to want that responsibility. Women, in spite of whatever flaws, weaknesses, or issues they may have, do bring unprecedented value to the table of life. Indeed, the power they possess is nothing to be taken lightly or ever taken for granted.

If you visit any of the most common business establishments such as grocery stores, clothing stores, jewelry stores, and shopping malls, you will find that those establishments typically have far more women patrons than men patrons. Establishments like sports arenas, electronic gadget venues, and X-rated establishments will typically have more men patrons. Notice that the three main types of establishments that cater to men also forms the acronym S.E.X. (**S**ports, **E**lectronics, and **X**-Rated) Oh yeah, did I mention Home Depot?

The High Cost of a Lap Dance

We find in *Mark 6:21* that King Herod offered the daughter of his illegitimate wife, Herodias, up to half of his kingdom. Notice too that the king was not asking for sex. He just wanted a lap dance and was willing to give the dancer up to half of his kingdom. I said half of his kingdom, not half of his paycheck or half of his house or half of his portfolio, but half of his kingdom, and all of that for one short lap dance.

She must have been one fine and beautiful woman or she must have had some dance moves that were out of this world. This woman had some extraordinary power. Her name could have been Wonder Woman, because she most certainly makes me wonder what kind of moves she possibly had, to make a king offer her half of his kingdom. Think about that. The king could have just commanded her to dance or paid her the customary fee for dancers. She really knew how to "make it rain". (Wow!)

Herod was afraid to kill John the Baptist because John was viewed as a prophet, and Herod was afraid that the people would be against him if he killed him. Nevertheless, at the request of this dancer, Herod did what he was otherwise so afraid to do. He had John beheaded.

Mark 6:21 And when a convenient day was come, that Herod on his birthday made a supper to his lords, high captains, and chief estates of Galilee;

Mark 6:22 And when the daughter of the said Herodias came in, and danced, and pleased Herod and them that sat with him, the king said unto the damsel, Ask of me whatsoever thou wilt, and I will give it thee.

Mark 6:23 And he swore unto her, Whatsoever thou shalt ask of me, I will give it thee, unto the half of my kingdom.

There is another dramatic Bible story that demonstrates even more plainly how awesome and crippling the power of a woman is. It helps us better understand what Adam was dealing with when he dealt with Eve.

I Am Sick and Tired of Your Mouth (The Story of Sampson and Delilah)

Judges 16:4 And it came to pass afterward, that he loved a woman in the valley of Sorek, whose name was Delilah.

Judges 16:5 And the lords of the Philistines came up unto her, and said unto her, Entice him, and see wherein his great strength lieth, and by what means we may prevail against him, that we may bind him to afflict him: and we will give thee every one of us eleven hundred pieces of silver.

Sampson was a very strong man, and men were powerless to subdue him. Finding themselves unable to conquer Sampson, they turned to a woman with whom Sampson had a love affair. Her name was Delilah. The Philistines contracted with Delilah to entice Sampson and find the source of his strength. Sampson repeatedly lied to Delilah until she was fed up with his lying.

Judges 16:16 *And it came to pass, when she pressed him daily with her words, and urged him, so that his soul was vexed unto death;*

Judges 16:17 *That he told her all his heart, and said unto her, There hath not come a razor upon mine head; for I have been a Nazarite unto God from my mother's womb: if I be shaven, then my strength will go from me, and I shall become weak, and be like any other man.*

Delilah apparently began to shut her legs and open her mouth delivering constantly nagging words. Every day she was at him, nagging and denying him sex. Sampson got to a point where he said, *"I can't take this crap no more. All right, I will tell you what you want to know. After I tell you the truth, I want you to shut your mouth and open your legs, so I can get my groove back. I am sick of you nagging me and denying me sex every day. I can't take this!"* Men often go along with what their woman wants or says to keep the peace or get a piece, and usually it's both that men want.

Delilah, using the power of a nagging tongue coupled with the power of sexual denial, conquered the mighty Sampson. When Sampson went to sleep, she gave him a messed-up haircut and when Sampson awakened, he was weaker than a crackhead. Indeed, with that jacked-up haircut, he looked like a crackhead. All his power was gone. Although a woman is usually physically weaker than a man, she has great power to make a man do certain things. A man will do irrational and detrimental things to have peace and to get a piece. A woman sometimes can be difficult to live with, and challenging to live without.

Now I know some of you are saying, "the Scripture didn't say anything about her denying him sex" and you are right. But think about it though. Do you really think that Sampson revealed the secret of his power just to stop her nagging? I know that a nagging woman can get on a man's last nerves, but usually when a woman is nagging a man that much, he either stays away all the time and sleeps in the guest bedroom or on the couch when he is home, or he leaves the woman altogether.

Now, for Sampson to stay home and put up with her irritating nagging, she had to be giving him some good loving that Sampson was not ready to walk away from. In addition, you all know, that when a woman is upset or being denied something she really wants badly, she will shut down the candy store until further notice. (Those of you who are married know exactly what I am talking about). Some things you just have to read between the lines and use common sense to understand.

Adam was dealing with the same thing, the power of a woman. Eve more than likely used her seductive power to suggest to Adam how good she was going to make him feel if he did what she wanted him to do or if he did not do it, how vexed up and miserable he was going to be from not having access to her body. Almost everything becomes irrelevant or invisible to a man when a man's mind is intently focused on sex. He automatically switches from thinking with his upper head, and is led by his lower head.

Consider men like Bill Clinton, Jim Baker, Jimmy Swaggart, and others. These men were at the top of their game when they were overcome by the seductive power of a woman. They were driven by their own lust, but the woman had the power to capitalize on that weakness. It is amazing how men of great stature will risk losing what took them years to attain just to fulfill a sexual fantasy with a woman in a fleeting moment.

The Wisest Man Became a Fool for Sex

In Solomon's time, there was no man alive as rich, powerful, and wise as King Solomon. King Solomon, although blessed with unprecedented wisdom, foolishly built pagan shrines for his foreign wives and allowed them to influence him to turn his heart away from God and worship idols. God warned him on a couple of occasions not to indulge his foreign women. In spite of all the wisdom God had blessed him with, Solomon nevertheless ignored God and yielded to his jungle fever.

1 Kings 11:1 *Now King Solomon loved many foreign women. Besides Pharaoh's daughter, he married women from Moab, Ammon, Edom, Sidon, and from among the Hittites.*

1 Kings 11:2 *The LORD had clearly instructed the people of Israel, 'You must not marry them, because they will turn your hearts to their gods.' Yet Solomon insisted on loving them anyway.*

1 Kings 11:3 *He had 700 wives of royal birth and 300 concubines. And in fact, they did turn his heart away from the LORD.*

1 Kings 11:4 *In Solomon's old age, they turned his heart to worship other gods instead of being completely faithful to the LORD his God, as his father, David, had been.*

1Kings 11:5 Solomon worshiped Ashtoreth, the goddess of the Sidonians, and Molech, the detestable god of the Ammonites.

1Kings 11:6 In this way, Solomon did what was evil in the LORD's sight; he refused to follow the LORD completely, as his father, David, had done.

1Kings 11:7 On the Mount of Olives, east of Jerusalem, he even built a pagan shrine for Chemosh, the detestable god of Moab, and another for Molech, the detestable god of the Ammonites.

1Kings 11:8 Solomon built such shrines for all his foreign wives to use for burning incense and sacrificing to their gods.

1Kings 11:9 The LORD was very angry with Solomon, for his heart had turned away from the LORD, the God of Israel, who had appeared to him twice.

1Kings 11:10 He had warned Solomon specifically about worshiping other gods, but Solomon did not listen to the LORD's command.

1Kings 11:11 So now the LORD said to him, "Since you have not kept my covenant and have disobeyed my decrees, I will surely tear the kingdom away from you and give it to one of your servants.

1Kings 11:12 But for the sake of your father, David, I will not do this while you are still alive. I will take the kingdom away from your son.

1Kings 11:13 And even so, I will not take away the entire kingdom; I will let him be king of one tribe, for the sake of my servant David and for the sake of Jerusalem, my chosen city."

Solomon was indeed a godly wise man and highly favored by God, but once again, the vagina trumped obedience to God. If sex is what caused the wisest man ever to disobey God, I am quite certain that it is the same reason Adam disobeyed God. I rest my case. I don't know what God put in that hole that makes the most powerful of men disobey Him just to have access to a vagina. It almost seems like sex is more powerful than God. The reality is that many men are very weak in the flesh and love sex more than they love God. However, God always will have good men around that will obey him.

Examples of Overcomers: A Few Good Men

There are two familiar stories in the Bible of two men who did not succumb to the power of the woman. One was Job, and the other was Joseph. These two men when they were challenged by the influential power of a woman stood their ground. They remained faithful to God and resisted the women that, Satan was trying to use to bring them down and cause them to disobey God. These men were true men of God. They had impeccable integrity. They valued their right standing and untarnished relationship with God more than anything a woman or the world could offer them.

These two men demonstrated that although a woman is well equipped with, almost irresistible sensual weapons of mass seduction, and is capable of subduing most men, they were determined and resolved that they would not become a victim or casualty of that awesome power of a woman. Job told his wife, *"Look here, After all that I have just gone through, I am fully prepared to give you your walking papers. This is really the wrong time for you to start tripping. What you are telling me to do is going to cause me far greater problems than what I have already experienced. You are about to make me lose my religion. I seriously suggest that you get out of my face with that bull crap you are talking. You must be out of your rabbit mind to be telling me to curse God and die. You— do it!"*

His wife had seriously kindled his anger, but Job figured, he had already lost every thing else, and if his wife wanted to leave him at that point, then that one more calamity was not going to make much of any difference to him.

Joseph resolved in is mind that he had already suffered wrongly at the hands of his brothers, having done nothing wrong. He thought how much more would he suffer for doing something he was guilty of? He surmised if he had gone to bed with his master's wife, he would have ended up in a different type of prison. His master's wife would have kept him in bondage to her, and it just was not worth what that decision would ultimately cost him.

Job and Joseph were two classic examples of servants of God who experienced great adversities for no apparent good reason. This is a very difficult thing to go through. It is very baffling when you are striving diligently to please God, obeying him to the best of your ability, and living as holy and righteously as you know how, and all manner of evil still invades your life.

When you are going through something like that, you begin to wonder if you have done something that has sorely displeased God. You cry out to God, *"I know that I am not perfect, but I am pressing toward the mark of perfection. I am seriously trying to do right by you. Why are you allowing me to go through these unnecessary changes? You said that you would supply all my needs.*

You promised to keep me in all my ways. Where are you? Why have you not rescued your servant from these evils?"

Job and Joseph were two true men of God, and yet God allowed them to experience harsh evils in spite of their righteous living. Not only did he allow these two men of God to suffer trials and tribulations, he suffered many of his other servants like the prophets, John the Baptist, Paul, and even his only begotten Son Jesus to endure suffering for righteousness' sake. Why would a loving God allow his children and faithful servants to go through such terrible dark valleys of evil?

That is an interesting and fair question, and one that many faithful saints would like to understand. If you get chastised for doing wrong or have to serve time in prison for breaking the law, that is your just reward for doing evil. You got what you rightfully deserve. But if you are chastised or imprisoned for something you did not do or for doing right, that result is both unjust and wrongful. Therefore, when God allows the righteous to suffer evil, it seems to be unjust and incomprehensible. Why would God allow such evil to prevail against a faithful servant who is living righteously? It almost doesn't make any sense.

I have previously told you that the answers to life's problems are found in the Word of God. The reason why God allows the good to suffer evil is found in the Scriptures below.

1 Peter 2:19 (NLT) *For God is pleased with you when you do what you know is right and patiently endure unfair treatment.*

1 Peter 2:20 *Of course, you get no credit for being patient if you are beaten for doing wrong. But if you suffer for doing good and endure it patiently, God is pleased with you.*

1 Peter 2:21 *For God called you to do good, even if it means suffering, just as Christ suffered for you. He is your example, and you must follow in his steps.*

1 Peter 2:22 *He never sinned, nor ever deceived anyone.*

1 Peter 2:23 *He did not retaliate when he was insulted, nor threaten revenge when he suffered. He left his case in the hands of God, who always judges fairly.*

Romans 5:3 (NLT) *We can rejoice, too, when we run into problems and trials, for we know that they help us develop endurance.*

Romans 5:4 *And endurance develops strength of character, and character strengthens our confident hope of salvation.*

Romans 5:5 *And this hope will not lead to disappointment. For we know how dearly God loves us, because he has given us the Holy Spirit to fill our hearts with his love.*

God wants us to do what is right even when it costs us for doing so. I know that is a hard pill for many to swallow. It's tight but it's right. The whole idea is that when we do what is right, it exemplifies the character of God, and God rewards us for obeying Him rather than obeying the devil or our flesh. When we do what is right, we are trusting God to make any wrong done to us right.

When we are consistently living right and God allows us to suffer or experience evil, He is validating us and purifying us. Trials and tribulations represent spiritual fire. Intense fire is used to purify precious metals. God sees us as gold, but in order for gold to be of great value and useful, it needs to be purified by fire. So in a like way, God allows us to be subjected to trials and tribulations, so He can burn away the evil in our lives and cause us to come forth as pure gold and radiate his glory ever more.

God will not leave us or forsake us. I know that sometimes it looks as though He has forsaken us, but in reality, everything that we go through is working in tandem to ultimately produce a good outcome for us. When we look at the end of the stories of Job, Joseph, and Jesus, we see that at certain points in all their lives, it looked like God had forsaken them. But when we look at the end of their stories, we see clearly that God used the bad to bring forth something very good.

Each of these examples demonstrates that God will allow righteous people that truly obey and serve Him, to suffer many evils when they have not done anything evil to deserve such suffering. Nevertheless, God brings them through it, perfects them, and blesses them. Conversely, we see others like Paul, John the Baptist, the prophets, and the other apostles who suffered even unto death. Instead of God delivering them from death, He delivered them by death. They lived and suffered for the cause of Christ. They laid down their lives, so that we would have their example and testimony to build our own faith upon.

Many who live godly lives will not see prosperity and a life of ease. Some believers will experience a life of suffering for righteousness because of their calling and their purpose in God's plan. However, the rewards that await them will dramatically outweigh the suffering they were allowed to endure in this life.

Will You Let the Dog, or the God In You, Control Your Behavior?

George Clinton said, *"Why must I chase the cat? Why must I be like that? It's nothing but the dog in me"*. The dog-like spirit in men is what makes them fall prey to the temptation of cat chasing. Men like Adam and Sampson disobeyed God and forfeited their blessings, because of the D-O-G that was in them. It was the G-O-D in Job and Joseph, however, that made them obey God, and remain faithful to Him, resulting in their being abundantly blessed. Henceforth, every man must decide whether he is going to continue to be a Dog-man or become a true God-man.

Cat Women Are On the Prowl

As for women, many have become just like dogs. In today's world, the cat is chasing the dog. Women today are letting it all hang out. They are wearing skintight clothes and clothes that draw attention to all their alluring and enticing body parts. Their skimpy and tight-fitting garments are their way of formatting their body parts. Certain parts are highlighted, some get underlined, some are highlighted in **bold prints**, and some are *italicized*. They want to make sure you get the message loud and clear with an emphasis on certain high interest and captivating parts.

Their tight clothes accentuate every curve, crack, and cranny. It whispers to men, *"Check out my big butt, my voluptuous breasts, and my sexy camel toe"*. If you are driving, you have to be careful not to swerve as your eyes travel the course of their winding curves that are almost demanding that you look at them. It is as if they are walking billboards for sexual services. It is as though they are silently yelling out by the way they are dressed. *"Attention all dogs, calling all dogs, free sex available here"*. Yet in a small unspoken voice, there is a fine print message that says: *(Some terms and conditions apply)*. That means, this woman has some bills that need to be paid, and Christmas is coming, and her kids will need you to play Santa Claus.

Many women today have become Cat-women, and they are chasing after Batman. They are subtly saying to Batman by advertising all their voluptuous goods, *"Come hit this"*. Some are doing it for financial reasons, some because of low self-esteem, some because they just love having sex, and some are just outright, whores, freaks, and nymphomaniacs.

Be Filled With the Spirit

The major problem with all of this is that God purposely created women in such a way that by design, they are fascinating, enticing, intriguing, and tempting human vessels. Then women take the awesome package that God has endowed them with, and take it to, a whole nother level. They put on make-up, sexy clothes, sexy hairstyles, paint their fingers and toenails, and put on ornamental jewelry to further enhance their beauty. Then they top all that off with alluring fragrances. (This is why it takes women so doggone long to get dressed.)

It is almost like a set-up. God hardwires a man to desire sex and desire a woman, and then He designs women with a full package of irresistible parts. Then they adorn themselves in a way to make themselves even more enticing, beautiful, and irresistible, and God gives the man a command not to have sex with them unless he is married to her.

A man has to be immersed in the Holy Spirit in order to obey this command consistently and faithfully. I guess that is the whole idea that God is trying to get across to us. A man needs to be totally sold out to God and filled and overflowing with the Holy Spirit in order to obey God in all things. There are some serious temptations in this world, especially women, and it is impossible to live "for real holy" without being immersed in the Holy Ghost.

Variety Is the Spice of Life, But Only Choose One

We all have an appetite for food and for sex. In the food world, God has created all kinds of delicious and desirable foods for consumption and has given humans the ability to create all sorts of appetizing dishes and recipes. What if God gave a command that we had to choose only one thing that we could eat and had to eat only that food for the rest of our lives? Not only would this be a very difficult decision to make; it would be torturous to deny ourselves the pleasure of enjoying all the other delectable foods that are available.

Similarly, this is the idea God has established concerning women. There are so many beautiful and desirable women in this world, and each one have her own unique look, taste, smell, touch, feel, and way of making a man feel like he is experiencing heaven on earth.

Unlike food, man is commanded by God to choose one woman and only have sex and intimacy with her for the rest of his life. Therefore, a man has to learn to control his God-given sexual desires and only satisfy them with the woman to whom he is married. This is a major challenge for most men, and God set this whole thing up like this for a reason.

What's Love Got To Do With It?

This whole thing is about love. It is about whom or what you love the most. Do you love God the most, do you love money the most, or do you love women and sex the most? God is the greatest of the three, and God is the one who created the concept of money and He also created the woman. But the big problem is that most men and women love money and sex more than they love God. God's challenge to us and His desire for us is to love Him far more than we love anything else, including the sex and the money He created for us.

God states that if you love Him, you prove and demonstrate it by doing what He commands us to do. Therefore, if we allow sex, money, or anything else, to influence or persuade us to disobey God's Word, that is evidence that our love for that other thing, is greater than our love for God. When your love for God is truly greater, you will do as Joseph and as Jesus did. You will resist the temptation and be fully obedient to the Word of God.

God presented man with something called woman to challenge man's love and obedience toward Him. He purposely made a woman such an awesome and compelling creature to determine if man would love God more than he would love a woman. This is probably the greatest challenge for most men.

I have lived on earth for fifty-nine years to date, and sex with a woman is the closest thing I have experienced on earth that I can imagine being what I envision a heavenly experience would be like. I imagine, that Heaven offers experiences, far beyond anything we have or will experience on earth. Nevertheless, I believe that God lets us experience the joy and pleasure of sex to give us a foretaste of His Glory divine.

Have you noticed that all too often when humans have really good sex, throughout that experience, they invoke the name of Jesus and repeatedly say stuff like, *"Oh My God!"* I am not just talking about believers. Hardcore sinners do this too. (I know because I use to be one.) Even atheists say OMG, when they are experiencing good sex and supposedly, they do not believe there is a God. Good sex from an earthly perspective is an experience that is second to none! Praise God, amen!

It's All About the Benjamins

Women love money because women love stuff (shoes in particular), and money buys the stuff they want and love. Men love sex with women (I know there is that segment of the male population that love sex with men, but right now, I am dealing with men who are normal). So as I was saying, normal men love having sex with women.

One of the things that motivate women to have sex with men is money or being showered with the things money can buy. (I know that sounds like prostitution, probably because indirectly, it is.) If a woman's primary or only reason for having sex with a man is to be rewarded with money or the things that money can buy, then she is in principle, a prostitute, regardless of what she calls herself.

Some women are upfront about their prostitution, and you know that when you encounter them. They are in the business of selling sex. They typically stand on street corners, inform you upfront what is on the menu and how much it will cost and make you fully aware that it is strictly a business transaction for them. They do not waste time trying to establish an intimate relationship with you. The only relationship they are interested in, is a business relationship. (You got the money, she's got the honey; let's hit it, quit it. "See you next time" is their motto and mantra.)

Other women pretend to love you and pretend to be in a love relationship with you, but it is really still all about the Benjamins. You will know when you have one of these undercover prostitutes (also known as golddiggers), because, when the money is gone, so is she. When the Benjamins stop flowing, so does the sex. Unfortunately, this is also true of some women who even wear the title called 'wife'.

Dollar bills and credit cards are forms of currency. Money is a means of exchange. Money can be anything used in exchange for goods and services. Therefore, almost anything can serve as money. When the world once operated on a barter system, everything a person possessed was money. Some men will do or give up almost anything and everything to get laid, and some women will do or give up anything and everything to get paid.

Love Not the World

1John 2:15 Love not the world, neither the things that are in the world. If any man love the world, the love of the Father is not in him.

1 John 2:16 *For all that is in the world, the lust of the flesh, and the lust of the eyes, and the pride of life, is not of the Father, but is of the world.*

1 John 2:17 *And the world passeth away, and the lust thereof: but he that doeth the will of God abideth for ever.*

The word 'love' in this context denotes *taking pleasure in the thing, prizing it above other things, and is unwilling to abandon it or do without it.* It conveys the idea of *having high esteem and placing great value on something to the point that you will die for it, forsake God, disobey God, or even do evil to get or keep it.*

When we love any material thing as much or more than we love God, we make that thing more important and more valuable than God, and that is idolatry and spiritual adultery. The way we know if we love something more than God is when we choose to do something wrong over doing what is right and pleasing to God. We spend most of our time and resources that God has blessed us with to chase after vanity and worldly lusts and neglect to pursue and support the things of God. We misuse and abuse people for material gain and to fulfill our fleshy desires.

Loving Your Fellowman Demonstrates You Love God

God gives all good things to us to use and enjoy. However, He never told us to love material things. On the contrary, He told us in numerous places throughout Scriptures, to love our fellow humans. God wants us to love people and responsibly use things. We have somehow got that point of view twisted around. We love things and irresponsibly use people.

Human beings are a physical representation of God. We were created in the image and likeness of God. That is why the Scriptures say, *"If a man say, I love God, and hates his brother, he is a liar: for he that loves not his brother whom he hath seen, how can he love God whom he hath not seen?" (**1 John 4:20**)*

God is trying to get us to understand the correlation between God and man. In other words, He wants us to understand that we demonstrate our love for the invisible God by showing love to the entity that was created in His image and made as a physical representation of the invisible God. That entity is humanity.

That is why Jesus said in ***Mathew 22:37-39***, answering the question: Which is the great commandment in the law?

Jesus said unto him, Thou shalt love the Lord thy God with all thy heart, and with all thy soul, and with all thy mind. This is the first and great commandment. And the second is like unto it, Thou shalt love thy neighbor as thyself. **(Mathew 22:37-39)**

He is clearly indicating that the two most important concerns of God for humanity is to love Him wholeheartedly and love our fellowman by treating them in the same way we want to be treated. When we do that, we demonstrate that we love the God we cannot see. You cannot truly fulfill the first commandment without first fulfilling the second one. Abiding by the second commandment technically fulfills the first commandment by default.

CHAPTER SEVEN
A Walk On The Wild Side:
Evil Gets Progressively Worse As It Advances

Role Reversal and Redefining Marriage

Over the course of time, there has been a radical role reversal for men and women. Some men are acting like women, and some women are behaving like a man. This role reversal is reflected in sexual behavior, the primary breadwinner role, and who takes care of the children and does the cooking and cleaning around the house.

Satan always strives to pervert, twist, or flip the script on whatever God has ordained and established. That is why we see today the institution of marriage being challenged and even redefined. God established that marriage should only be between a man and a woman. He established Adam and Eve, as that marriage union model.

However, all that is changing. Marriage is being redefined as a legal union between two people. Under this definition, any two people can be married without regard to gender. Under this perversion, instead of having Adam and Eve as the only marriage model, the world has introduced two new models. It can now be Adam and Steve, or Adah and Eve.

To add insult to injury, there is another perverted concept under way called polyamorous relationships. This arrangement is a hybrid of polygamy (having multiple spouses) and these spouses can be any combination of heterosexual and homosexual participants. For example: A ployamorous relationship can consist of three males and five females with all being bisexual. If you think that we have serious issues and problems with a monogamous relationship between one man and one woman, just wait until the crap hits the fan in a polyamorous relationship.

This is a diabolical recipe for chaos and disaster, and the implications are indeed far reaching. The devil will stop at nothing. As in the days of Noah, the thoughts and behavior of humans are becoming progressively and increasingly vile, wicked, and perverted.

In the movement to sanctify same sex marriages, the issue seems to evolve around and focus on sexual preferences and same sex couples being able to enjoy the benefits and privileges granted to heterosexual marriages. When we consider why God created the institution of marriage in the first place, we can better understand why He restricted it to one man and one woman. God established marriage between a man and a woman because His purpose was to enable procreation and the multiplication of animal species through sexual intercourse.

I said 'species' because we do see that across the board, God created most if not all species of animals to procreate through sexual intercourse with the opposite, not the same sex. He established this principle throughout nature. Same sex individuals cannot procreate. A man cannot have a baby, and a woman cannot get another woman or a man pregnant. God intended procreation to happen through the natural means of sexual intercourse, not by any scientific or technological means.

Many people think that sex is just for pleasure and enjoyment. No doubt, sex is very pleasurable and enjoyable, but that is not its primary purpose. Pleasure certainly is a benefit of sex and is precisely what entices us to engage in it repeatedly. If sex were not a highly desirable and pleasurable activity, most of us would not desire it and thus do it frequently. Furthermore, many of us would likely not have children. A large percentage of the children that have resulted from sexual intercourse were not planned. They were the results of two people enjoying sex most likely without protection, and pregnancy was the unplanned result.

The concept of family was the intended goal of procreation. God wanted this family to be created in the context of a marriage between the only two entities He designed for procreation, which are a man and a woman. According to the Law of God, marriage was intended to be a lifetime covenant and commitment between a man and a woman and made legally binding by an act of human law.

What homosexuals are trying to do is change both the Law of God and the law of man. They may attain success in changing the law of man; however, there is absolutely nothing anyone can do to change the

Law of God! What God has established, no one can change. If man's law were to make it lawful to shed innocent blood, that would not change the Law of God and God still would hold everyone accountable to His Law regardless of what man's law allows that, is contrary to God's Law.

All Sex Outside of Marriage Is Fornication

Homosexuals want their perverted lifestyle to be sanctioned by law. The only act of sexual intercourse related to humans that God sees as acceptable, holy, righteous, and sanctified by Him is sex between a legally married man and woman. Any other sexual intercourse engaged by humans is classified as fornication, except when a legally married man or woman has sex with someone other than their legal spouse. That is classified as adultery. Therefore, all sex between unmarried individuals of the opposite sex, same sex, animals, angels, or any combination or variation of these arrangements, is considered fornication and forbidden by God.

Let me make this very clear. Sex between unmarried heterosexuals is just as much a sin as sex between homosexuals or sex that is adultery. One cannot rightfully point the finger at the other. The only difference between them, is that sexual desire for the opposite sex is natural and hardwired into humans by God. It is just as natural as humans desiring food when they are hungry and drink when they are thirsty. However, things that are unnatural, contrary to God's laws, and contrary to His design, are what God considers to be perversions, abnormal use, and thus of the devil.

Everyone needs food and water to live. However, we can live without things like illegal drugs, cigars, cigarettes, alcoholic beverages, and many of other vices that people become addicted to easily. The point is that there are certain things that virtually all humans normally and naturally desire and need. There are also many unnatural desires, that some people elect to consume or engage in. Typically, these elective vices cause problems and harm to those that indulge them and sometimes to others.

Nevertheless, things that are natural and permitted by God can also be misused and abused. Although it is permitted by God to enjoy whatever food and drink we desire, too much of certain good things can become harmful and hazardous to our health. For example, eating too much food containing sugars and salt or not eating enough foods that contain essential vitamins and nutrients can result in adverse health conditions. Eating good food is good, but eating an excessive amount of good food is gluttony and leads to obesity and adverse health conditions.

If you habitually practice sinning as a lifestyle, it is evident that you are living contrary to the Law and Will of God. God's Grace is given to us as a demonstration of His love and kindness and a window of opportunity to get right with Him. However, if we abuse that grace and use it as a license to continue in our sinful ways, our time will eventually expire, and if at such time you are still living a sinful lifestyle, you will face the consequences and receive your just reward at the appointed time.

Do not play games with God or take His grace for granted or as a license to continue in sin. God's grace is given to help those who are striving to do right by God. It is not a loophole in the system to be used by gamers to game the system. You cannot run game on God. If you try to run game on God, you are the one that is going to get played. God sees, hears, and knows everything, and if you think that, you can out smart Him, you had better think again.

Homosexuals Want to Redefine Marriage to Redefine Family
Homosexuals want to redefine marriage as a legal union between two adults. This definition will allow two adults of the same sex to legally be married and have all the benefits and rights afforded to heterosexual marriages. The premises of this concept is that their sexual preference and tendency is for the same sex, and so they feel they should be able to engage in a legal love relationship and be recognized and treated like any other legally married couple is treated.

Some of the potential ramifications of redefining marriage are: it sets a precedent for future, even more perverted arguments. All other people who want to sanction their perverted relationship, will use this ruling as a basis for their own fight to attain what they want. This will set a precedent for people who want to legalize polygamy, polyandry, marriages between adults and minors, marriages between sibling and blood relatives, marriages between humans and their pets, and polyamorous marriages.

Ultimately, nothing will be off limits, and the concept of a traditional family will be dramatically redefined or even extinguished. A family will be redefined as: *"Any group of people bound together by a legal decree."* If this happens, a family will be any configuration that one wants it to be.

People will get very creative, legally form all sorts of legal marriages and families, and then legally claim rights and benefits granted to married status unions and family members of that union.

In the days of Noah, there was no law. People did whatever wicked and perverted thing they imagined, resulting in the destruction of all humans, excluding Noah and his family. Changing laws to sanction perversions and immoralities of people is as bad as having no laws at all. Having good laws in place lets us live in a civil society and experience a reasonable degree of order and sanity. When we begin to degrade the moral laws of our society, the degradation of the civil laws will eventually follow.

The original intent of God was to have a family unit consisting of a man and a woman legally married which produces offsprings through sexual intercourse. God intended the parents to teach their children the ways of God and teach them to love and obey God by both His precepts and their example. Many heterosexual couples have failed to meet this mandate, and yet some have done well.

If we had a society that has predominantly homosexual relationships, the only way for procreation to take place would be by using surrogates, science, and technology. Obviously, two men could not produce a child between the two of them only, and likewise, two women could not make that happen either. In such relationships, the children could only be adopted children. One of the parties in the marriage could be a sperm donor or in the case of two women, one could receive a sperm injection. However, the resulting child would not be biologically an offspring of both of them. Such a birth would require a third party and possibly scientific and technological assistance as well.

I have met and known several homosexuals, both male and female. They are no different from the rest of us in terms of their general human traits and abilities. Their mannerisms may sometimes be a little strange and different, but overall, just like heterosexuals, there are the good and not so good. They see their sexual behavior as a sexual preference. Choosing a chocolate cake over a vanilla cake is a preference. Choosing another man as your sexual partner is a perversion.

What we do with our bodies becomes a perversion when we do things with our bodies that God has clearly declared to be sinful, harmful, or wrong. Spiritually and morally speaking, fornication, homosexuality, incest, bestiality, and adultery are all sinful and wrong. No matter how we dress it up or try to redefine it, it is still sin. If you dress a pig in a beautiful dress, high heel shoes, and put makeup on him, he will still be a pig. Homosexuals need to stop trying to reduce their sin to just a personal sexual preference and realize that it is sexual immorality and a lifestyle that God does not approve of, or sanction.

Cultural Changes Do Not Change the Word of God

Many women today, think and feel that, because they make more money than their husbands, this qualifies them to be in charge and head of the marriage union. The head and leader of a marriage relationship is not defined or determined by who makes the most money or who is the most educated. That has nothing to do with it. (Nada) It is defined and determined by what God declares in his Word.

In the world and according to human rationale, whoever has the gold makes the rules. This may seem right and reasonable with respect to business, but that is not the case in marriage. According to worldly standards and practices, this practice may be indeed acceptable and applicable. However, in Christ and from God's perspective, it does not work like that in marriage.

This example relates to the core principle and idea I am trying to get across in this book. When God establishes a rule or law, it is not up for debate or revision based on cultural norms, practices, or how times have changed. Times may change, but God's immutable laws do not change. If God makes an unconditional law, it is not subject to personal or societal circumstances, beliefs, or opinions, and it is not up for a majority vote by the people. When God commanded that wives are to submit themselves to their own husbands as unto the Lord, He meant just that. He did not add any terms and conditions about which spouse makes the most money.

But let me qualify that statement a bit more. God may say one thing in a certain place in the Bible and may say another thing elsewhere in the Bible that relates to what He said in the first instance. An example of that potential confusion is: In one place, God commands believers *to submit to every authority and to submit to every ordinance of man*. But in another place, he instructs us *to obey God rather than man*.

What this difference means is that in general we should obey every ordinance and law of man, as the Lord has commanded. However, God also said that *every power is ordained of God and every power is subject to the higher power, and all powers are subject to God Almighty*.

Therefore, if a certain person or entity in authority is commanding or trying to force those under their authority to do or say something that violates the Supreme Law of God; in such case, *God commands us to obey His supreme law rather than to submit to a law or command of man that contradicts or is out of alignment with God's Supreme Law.*

Let me put that concept in more context. If your husband wants you to sell your body or participate in wife swapping or a sex orgy, you should not obey him or submit to that request. He is abusing his authority in doing so. He is asking you to do something that the Supreme Law of God has commanded you not to do. God's Law says, *"You should not commit adultery"*. There is nowhere in the Bible where it is written, that if your spouse does it, it is okay for you to do it. There is no passage in the Bible that says if both of you agree to have sex with other sex partners, it is acceptable to God.

Adultery is any form of sex with someone other than your legal spouse. Therefore, if he wants you to engage in any kind of sex with anyone else besides him, God sees that as an act of adultery and flat out forbids it. No ifs, ands, or buts, about it. So if you are doing so now, you need to repent and re-sanctify your marriage.

Therefore, if your husband whom God has ordained as head and leader of the marriage and the household, demands anything that is clearly forbidden by God, you are not, I repeat, you are NOT, obligated to submit to that demand or obey him. In such a case, you are commanded *to obey God rather than man*. This rule applies to any authoritative figure, including your husband, your pastor, your boss, the police, your government, or the President. They are all subject to God and will ultimately answer to Him.

Two classic examples in Scripture are Daniel in the Lion's den and the three Hebrews; Shadrach, Meshach, and Abednego in the fiery furnace. These men of God had to make a life or death decision to obey God or obey man. In these two situations, the king decreed that whoever did not obey what he commanded them to do; they would be brutally put to death.

Normally, these men of God would have obeyed the king as they should and as they normally did. However, in these particular situations, the king was commanding them to do something that God had commanded that the men of God were forbidden by God to do. God had an ordinance that forbade them to bow down to any graven image or pray to any other god than God Almighty. The king was commanding that they do both of these things.

These men of God had to make a decision to obey God or obey the king. They chose to obey God and let the chips fall wherever they may. They were willing to suffer whatever consequences went with obeying God. The consequence of these two situations was death by cruel and unusual punishment. They obeyed God and gladly accepted that fate. Needless to say, they stayed true and faithful to God, and God in turn stayed true and faithful to them. God then delivered them from death and spared their lives.

When we are faced with challenges wherein a human authority has commanded us to do something that God has directly and explicitly forbidden, we have to make a critical decision between obeying God or obeying man. In these situations, we must obey God and trust God to deliver us, even unto death. *"To be absent from the body is to be present with the Lord"*, and that is a good thing.

The Carnal and Spiritual Alliance with Man and Woman
What is going on today is the same exact thing that was going on in the Garden of Eden. It was all about a man who had authority (the right to rule, a woman who had the power to influence the one that had the right to rule, and the devil, the spiritual force that has the power to deceive the woman who has the power to influence the man who was authorized to rule the earth). This is the carnal alliance. When these three work together, whether done intentionally or not, they will cause the will of Satan, not God's Will, to prevail on earth.

When the man and the woman work in harmony with the Spirit of God, they cause the Will of God to be accomplished. This is the spiritual alliance. When God wants to accomplish something on earth, He goes to the man and makes known His Will. The man is then responsible for telling his wife what God said. The woman's responsibility is to help the man accomplish what God instructed him to do.

When Satan wants to accomplish his will on earth, he goes to the woman first and tells her what he wants to make happen. After he sells the woman on the idea, he relies on the woman to work her magic and influence the man to go along with the program. This is reverse order.

A woman is uniquely equipped to assist a man in being successful in life and providing him with the support, encouragement, and comfort that he needs. A woman has far more to offer than just sexual services.

She has intelligence, skills, insight, advice, and many other assets. There is an old adage that says, behind every successful man, is a good woman, and it is true in most cases.

The woman must choose whether she is going to use her God-given power to build up and support the God-inspired vision and goals given to her husband, or use her power to tear him down and reduce him to a spiritual wimp.

CHAPTER EIGHT
It's All in the Mind

The Symptoms of a Much Bigger Internal Problem

Surely, there are a multitude of problems and evils manifested in the world. However, those evils are mere symptoms of a much larger internal problem. The evils we see on the outside are reflections and products of the evils abiding internally in the minds and hearts of humans. From within and from the abundance of what is stored in our hearts, is where all the evils we see in the world actually come from. From the heart come adultery, fornication, envy, strife, murder, contentions, wars, and a host of other evil activities.

Our heart is our spiritual hard drive, where all our spiritual data and applications are stored. Our mind accesses this stored information, and uses it to produce and manifest the things we issue into life. Therefore, if we have problems and negative issues in our life, it means that we have problems and evil agendas in our heart that we need to eradicate in order to eliminate the problems and drama manifested in our daily lifestyle.

How Does the Virus of Evil Corrupt Our Heart?

Now that we understand where the evils we see manifested in our world come from, next we need to understand how evil gets there. Were we born with it, or did we acquire it from some external source? It's an important question. Well, when we look back at Adam and Eve, and examine how their evil thought that led them to disobey God entered their minds and ended up in their hearts, we discover the source.

It all started with *Genesis 3:1* when the serpent (the devil, the spirit of evil and father of lies) began a conversation with Eve. The spirit of evil will always start this conversation. The devil communicates a thought to your mind. That thought may come as an idea, question, or suggestion, depending on what the devil wants at that time. Sometimes he wants you to doubt, disbelieve, and disobey God (that was the game plan with Adam and Eve). Other times, he is only trying to get you to turn away from God. However, sometimes his objective can be for you to use your mind and body to carry out his evil work.

We Cannot Serve Two Masters

Mathew 6:24 (NLT) No one can serve two masters. For you will hate one and love the other; you will be devoted to one and despise the other. You cannot serve both God and money.

Many times, the devil wants us to manifest his evil plan to demonstrate he is in control of our minds and bodies. When we do evil things, (anything contrary or out of alignment with the Word of God and the Spirit of Love) we clearly show who we are obeying, worshipping, and serving, even if only for a moment.

We cannot serve two masters. We will of necessity, show more loyalty, dedication, and faithfulness to one over the other. The devil is fine with the idea of our serving him and God simultaneously. Conversely, God rejects this diabolical idea of serving two masters. The devil does not require exclusive worship. He is content to have us as a part-time lover, which is unacceptable to God, and sorely displeases God. God proclaims that *He is a jealous God,* and does not allow us to serve other gods.

It is just like either a husband or wife having a part-time lover. The part-time lover is usually happy with the arrangement, but the faithful spouse, finds it highly offensive and unacceptable. God is offended when we give access to our soul and body to another god, especially the devil. God sees all and knows all, so do not think for one moment that you are putting one over on him.

Don't Worry About a Thing

Mathew 6:25 (NLT) That is why I tell you not to worry about everyday life—whether you have enough food and drink, or enough clothes to wear. Isn't life more than food, and your body more than clothing?

God does not want our minds consumed with worrying about daily necessities. He has told us he is fully aware of what we need. He also assures us that we are far more important to him than the birds. Therefore, He reminds us that *if your Heavenly Father takes care of the needs of the birds, He will certainly take care of ours.*

When we worry about such things, we do not really trust God to supply all our needs. The real reason we worry in many cases is because we spend so much of our resources on foolishness and stuff we really don't need. We go deep into debt to buy all the stuff we want and end up falling short of enough money to pay for the things we actually do need. When that happens, we resort to worrying because we have no idea of how to make ends meet. Then we panic and resort to doing even more foolish, even evil, things to bail ourselves out of the mess we allowed the devil to talk us into in the first place. This is how the devil gets us into trouble.

Always Seek the Kingdom of God First
God told us to set as our priority in life, the seeking of the Kingdom of God and its righteousness and procure those things that are above and not what is on earth. Store up treasures in Heaven, not on earth. The devil influences us of course to do just the opposite. He suggests we seek after things on earth and not worry or concern ourselves with the spiritual. That is how we end up doing just as Adam and Eve did, and we obey the devil instead of obeying God.

Solomon said there is nothing new under the sun. Solomon was not referring to technological advancements; he was talking about the dumb stupid stuff humans keep doing. More than 6,000 years later, we are still stuck on stupid.

God Owns Your Body Exclusively
God has declared that our body belongs to Him alone, and it was made for His exclusive use. Therefore, He has commanded us to yield our bodies over to works of righteousness only. When we allow our bodies to be used for evil purposes, we are abusing God's property.

Our body does not belong to us. We are only a temporary custodian and caretaker of it. God expects us to respect his property and responsibly take care of it and use it for His Kingdom's purposes to bring praise, honor, and glory to Him only. Therefore, if we are not using the body that He has entrusted to us for that purpose, we are misusing His body.

I know many of us think and believe that the body that we live in, belongs to us. We think that it is ours. That is what the devil and our own ignorance have led us to believe. According to the Word of God, (the ultimate source of Divine reliable truth), we have been bought with a price. Jesus redeemed us by shedding his precious sinless blood. That was the price paid by Jesus to buy us back from the curse of the Law.

This is looking at ownership of our bodies from a spiritual legal perspective. However, if we go to the root of the idea, God is the One who made our body and He has declared emphatically, that *the earth belongs to the Lord, the fullness thereof, and all them that dwell in it*. He has declared that *all things are made by Him and for Him to fulfill His purposes*. From the perspective of worship, God declares *our body to be the temple of the Holy Ghost*.

When we ignore what God has proclaimed concerning the body we live in, we are telling God *"whatever"!* We are telling God, *"I don't care what you say. I am going to do whatever I want with this body because it is my body, and I can do as I please with it!"*

This is what so many people feel about the body they believe is theirs. Nevertheless, I am serving notice to you, that if that is what you believe, you have it totally twisted! You have bought into another one of the devil's lies and deceptions. Those who misuse and destroy God's body, God will also destroy. That is what God has declared!

We Want Everything Handed to Us on a Silver Platter

Many people believe that all they have to do, is name it and claim it, and what they want, will magically, or supernaturally happen. People are more than willing to take an initial step toward something they want, but after that first step, they want God to do the rest.

That system works well if you only want negative results, but if you desire positive outcomes, you have to do something that is quite different. If you want a yard that looks like a jungle, just get a yard, then sit back, relax, and do nothing. You'll get your jungle.

Romans 6:12 (NLT) Do not let sin control the way you live; do not give in to sinful desires.

Romans 6:13 (NLT) Do not let any part of your body become an instrument of evil to serve sin. Instead, give yourselves completely to God, for you were dead, but now you have new life. So use your whole body as an instrument to do what is right for the glory of God.

1Corinthians 3:16 (NLT) Don't you realize that all of you together are the temple of God and that the Spirit of God lives in you?

1Corinthians 3:17 (NLT) God will destroy anyone who destroys this temple. For God's temple is holy, and you are that temple.

1 Corinthians 6:19 (NLT) Don't you realize that your body is the temple of the Holy Spirit, who lives in you and was given to you by God? You do not belong to yourself,

1 Corinthians 6:20 (NLT) for God bought you with a high price. So you must honor God with your body.

Psalms 24:1 The earth is the LORD'S, and the fulness thereof; the world, and they that dwell therein.

Colossians 1:15 (NLT) Christ is the visible image of the invisible God. He existed before anything was created and is supreme over all creation,

Colossians 1:16 (NLT) for through him God created everything in the heavenly realms and on earth. He made the things we can see and the things we can't see—such as thrones, kingdoms, rulers, and authorities in the unseen world. Everything was created through him and for him.

It is very easy to walk down an aisle and repeat the marriage vows, say "I do", kiss the bride, and be pronounced man and wife. However, making that marriage work, and living happily together until death do you apart, takes work, time, and a lot of patience. It does not all magically fall into place. It may very well play out that way in the movies but in real life, that is not the case. (You better ask somebody).

Some people even think that salvation is also just walking up to the altar, repeating the sinner's prayer, getting baptized, and the devil will back away from you and let you live a holy and righteous life in peace. That is simply not how it works either. If you do those things, that is good. But the reality is the same as it is with getting married. That initial public ceremony was your declaration of commitment to a long-term relationship. That was the easy part. Living holy and righteously every day is the real challenge.

Once you make that commitment, it is time to put your faith in action and live out your confession. It is time to walk out your vow daily and live a lifestyle that honors and pleases God. It is time to demonstrate your newfound belief by obeying what God commands us to do via the Word of God. You cannot sit back and continue to live the lifestyle of sin you were previously living before you accepted Christ. If you continue to go down the same road you were already on, you will end up at the same place where you were headed earlier, which is in Hell. If you end up in Hell, it is not because God sent you there, but because, that is the road you chose to travel.

We Must Be Transformed

Some people think that joining and attending a church in and of itself is sufficient. But Scripture admonishes us to *be not conformed to this world: but to be transformed by the renewing of our mind, that we may prove (demonstrate) what is that good, and acceptable, and perfect, will of God. (Romans 12:2)* This verse tells us we need to change the way we live and re-educate our mind.

This transformation process takes time, commitment, and a lot of work. It does not all supernaturally happen just because you have received the Holy Ghost. The Holy Ghost was given to you to lead and guide you into all truth and also empower you to obey God's Word. The Holy Spirit will lead you to the water, but He is not going to make you drink it nor will He drink that water for you. That is your responsibility. We must responsibly study the Word of God, and as the Holy Spirit opens the eyes of our understanding further, we are commanded to do what it says and not be hearers only.

The War Zone Is Your Life, but the Battle Is In Your Mind

The war zone is the general area where fighting between two opposing forces engages. God and the devil are at war contending for control of your life. Your life is the war zone, but the critical battles for it are fought on the battlefield of your mind. Your mind is like the capital city in this battle. Gaining control of your mind gives the victor control of your life and that control wins the war.

God's desire is to control your entire life, whereas the devil's is content with only controlling certain key aspects of your life. The devil may attack your finances and cause you to live in poverty, but that circumstance does not affect your salvation. It will only cause you to experience lack and have many financial difficulties. The devil may attack your family, your marriage, your business, and your social relationships with your friends, and destroy them all. Your loss of these things will not affect your salvation unless you allow these adversities to cause you to turn away from God and from doing what is right and pleasing to God. Job experienced these very same torments, but it did not affect his servitude or his attitude toward God.

Ezekiel 18:26 when righteous people turn from their righteous behavior and start doing sinful things, they will die for it. Yes, they will die because of their sinful deeds.

Ezekiel 18:27 And if wicked people turn from their wickedness, obey the law, and do what is just and right, they will save their lives.

Ezekiel 18:28 They will live because they thought it over and decided to turn from their sins. Such people will not die.

Sexual Immorality Can Cause You to Curse Yourself

1 Corinthians 6:18 (NLT) Run from sexual sin! No other sin so clearly affects the body as this one does. For sexual immorality is a sin against your own body.

Sexual immorality can lead to idolatry, unwanted pregnancy, venereal disease, divorces, embarrassment, child support, jail time, and many other evil outcomes. God gets really angry about sexual immorality.

When King Balak hired Balaam to curse Israel and its people, he could not. Every time he opened his mouth to curse them, blessings flowed from his mouth instead. Although he could not curse them, there was still a way for them to bring a curse upon themselves. God had commanded the Israelites not to go after foreign women. However, the men of Israel caught jungle fever and went whoring after the Moabite women. That transgression caused God to place a curse upon Israel. God would not allow anyone to curse Israel, but Israel could, and did, bring a curse upon themselves, by what they did. Their disobedience brought a curse upon them.

This is no difference here than with Adam and Eve, Sampson, or us. Adam lost his authority and was evicted from Paradise by disobeying God. Sampson lost his mighty power by disobeying God. Lucifer lost his place and position in Heaven by rebelling against God. The Israelites were evicted from the Promised Land and taken into captivity for seventy years for rebelling and disobeying God. God did not take back what He had given them; they simply disqualified themselves by breaking God's laws.

Although God has blessed us and granted us salvation, like Adam, we can forfeit it all by disobeying God. If after being saved, we go back to practicing sin, we are like a dog returning to his vomit or a pig that has been washed and clean who then returns to waddling in the muck.

Salvation is by faith, but faith is not belief alone. It is both believing and doing what God says. He gives us certain things to do, and certain other things, not to do. If we obey what He has commanded, we have nothing to worry about. But if we continuously disobey God, we will disqualify ourselves and lose out. Much of the evil we experience internally, and the evils we bring on ourselves, is due to our lack of knowledge and our choice to be disobedient.

Numbers 25:1 *And Israel abode in Shittim, and the people began to commit whoredom with the daughters of Moab.*

Numbers 25:2 *And they called the people unto the sacrifices of their gods: and the people did eat, and bowed down to their gods.*

Numbers 25:3 *And Israel joined himself unto Baalpeor: and the anger of the LORD was kindled against Israel.*

Numbers 25:4 *And the LORD said unto Moses, Take all the heads of the people, and hang them up before the LORD against the sun, that the fierce anger of the LORD may be turned away from Israel.*

Numbers 25:7 *And when Phinehas, the son of Eleazar, the son of Aaron the priest, saw it, he rose up from among the congregation, and took a javelin in his hand;*

Numbers 25:8 *And he went after the man of Israel into the tent, and thrust both of them through, the man of Israel, and the woman through her belly. So the plague was stayed from the children of Israel.*

Numbers 25:9 *And those that died in the plague were twenty and four thousand.*

Numbers 25:10 *And the LORD spake unto Moses, saying,*

Numbers 25:11 *Phinehas, the son of Eleazar, the son of Aaron the priest, hath turned my wrath away from the children of Israel, while he was zealous for my sake among them, that I consumed not the children of Israel in my jealousy.*

When the devil cannot bring a curse upon your life through other means, he will most definitely pull his trump card on you, and that is sexual sin. Therefore, guard your affections. Sex is a second-hand emotion. You can control it. Do not let it control you. It is a mind over matter thing.

When you let your emotions take control, that is the moment when you just lost control. But if you let the mind stay in control, and let the Word and the Spirit of God control your mind, I guarantee that everything will be all right. We can be delivered from evil if we stop evil at the door and identify and discard all the evil lurking in our minds. Your mind is the door to your life. That is why Paul said, *"So then with the mind I myself serve the law of God; but with the flesh the law of sin."* **Romans 7:25**

Trials, Tribulations, and Temptations (The Pains and Pleasures of Life)

The devil uses trials and temptations to test us. Trials test our endurance and tolerance, whereas temptations test our resistance to evil. The devil uses temptations to try to make us fall into sin. Temptations typically are those things that make us feel good. Often it is something that feels good to us, but not always good for us. It is usually something we want or desire but something we should not mess with. Our objective as believers is not to yield to such temptations.

Yielding to temptations can cause us to experience certain problems that create drama, pain, suffering, and other undesirable issues and circumstances that produce evil effects in our lives. We are tempted when evil and lustful desires from within, want to be satisfied, or there is something externally triggering our carnal appetites. When we satisfy that appetite by doing evil, the result is sin.

James 1:14 But every man is tempted, when he is drawn away of his own lust, and enticed.

James 1:15 Then when lust hath conceived, it bringeth forth sin: and sin, when it is finished, bringeth forth death.

Trials, on the other hand, are external adversities and oppositions that come against us to frustrate, hassle, hinder, beat down, persecute, and thwart us. They often cause us pain, suffering, and setbacks. As believers, we have to stand up to such oppositions. Although most of us do not like pain and suffering, such trials often serve useful purposes in our lives. They can develop and strengthen us. They also can reveal our weaknesses and reveals specific things we need to pray about and work on or correct in our lives.

1 Peter 4:12 Beloved, think it not strange concerning the fiery trial which is to try you, as though some strange thing happened unto you:

1 Peter 4:13 But rejoice, inasmuch as ye are partakers of Christ's sufferings; that, when his glory shall be revealed, ye may be glad also with exceeding joy.

Rom 5:3 And not only so, but we glory in tribulations also: knowing that tribulation worketh patience;

Rom 5:4 And patience, experience; **and** *experience, hope:*

Rom 5:5 And hope maketh not ashamed; because the love of God is shed abroad in our hearts by the Holy Ghost which is given unto us.

James 1:3 Knowing this, that the trying of your faith worketh patience.

James 1:4 But let patience have her perfect work, that ye may be perfect and entire, wanting nothing.

The Son of God Designation Exam

Jesus was led by the Spirit of God into the wilderness to take the Son of God designation exam. The examination administrator was the devil. This exam determined whether Jesus was qualified to be called The Son of God.

Exam Part 1: The Flesh Test
Objective: (Can you consistently deny the flesh)

When Jesus arrived at the examination site in the wilderness, his first test or challenge was to see if he could survive in the wilderness for 40 days and nights without eating anything. After these 40 days and nights passed, Jesus had successfully passed part one of the exam. The purpose of the exam was to see if he could deny his flesh consistently for an extended period of time. Jesus passed this test with flying colors.

The two carnal appetites virtually every human have are a desire for physical food and a desire for sex. We can live without sex, but we need food to live and provide nourishment for our body. Nevertheless, we can go without food for an extended time. Denying our body food for an extended time is called fasting. Fasting can be both physically and spiritually beneficial.

These two appetites can cause difficult problems. Americans in particular eat too much food and the wrong foods. Consequently, many of us are unhealthy and obese. Our sexual appetite also can cause many problems when we do not control it.

When we engage in sexual immorality, it puts us at odds with God and potentially can lead to many other problems in our lives. When we control these two appetites and use wisdom in the exercising of our liberties pertaining to both sex and food, we minimize the evils that can result from irresponsible eating habits and sexual promiscuity.

Exam Part 2: Test of Right Priorities and Values
Objective: To see where your priorities are and what you value most.

When Jesus had completed the previous portion of the exam, his stomach was growling louder than an angry wild animal. He was hungrier than five bears.

The devil then said to him, *"I know you are starving and there is no food out here. If you are supposed to be the Son of God, then prove it by turning these stones into a steak dinner."*

Jesus replied, *"First of all, I don't have to prove jack to you, because I know that I am who the Word of God says I am".*

Then the devil said, *"Okay, then tell me Mr. Jesus, what is more important than providing nourishment for your body? For surely, if you do not eat something, you will die."*

Jesus responded by saying, *"Food for my soul is far more important than food for my body. The body will eventually perish with or without food, but the soul lives forever. Therefore, I must concern myself with nourishing my soul more than nourishing my body."*

"Man needs more than just physical food to live, but for man to live as God intended him to live, man must live by every word that first comes from the mouth of God. By doing so, man shall live and not die and have everlasting life."

Many of us spend our prime time in life working for food, material things, and the pleasures and comforts of this life, and we neglect to attend to the needs of our soul. Many souls are starving for the nourishment that can only come from the Word of God.

God wants us to be more concerned and attentive to our spiritual needs than we are to our physical needs. Our body and this world are temporal, and they both will come to an end. However, our soul is eternal and will spend eternity somewhere, either with the devil or with God. If we neglect to prepare our soul to be a resident in the Kingdom of God, when it is established on earth, by default, our soul will end up in the eternal lake of fire (whatever that is). What I do know is that it does not sound like a place where I want to be.

Exam Part 3: Test of the Ability to Rightly Divide the Word of Truth
Objective: Determines if you know how to correctly interpret and apply scriptural knowledge.

So the devil said to Jesus in the wilderness, *"Okay, you seem to be a very sharp young man, you know who you are, you have your priorities straight, and you know what to place the most value on. I have another challenge for you. I want to see if your God really has your back".*

Mathew 4:5 Then the devil took him up into the holy city, and set him on a pinnacle of the temple,

Mathew 4:6 And saith unto him, If you are the Son of God, cast yourself down: for it is written, He shall give his angels charge concerning thee: and in [their] hands they shall bear thee up, lest at any time thou dash thy foot against a stone.

Jesus then explained, *"I am quite familiar with that Scripture. It is in **Psalms 91:11 and 12**. But for me to cast myself down just to see if it works is very foolish. For it is written:"*

Deuteronomy 6:16 "Ye shall not tempt the LORD your God, as ye tempted him in Massah".

Surely, God provides safety and protection to His children, but His children are not to test Him by doing foolish things. What God says is not to be misinterpreted or taken out of context. Some things that God says are superseded by other things that He says. Therefore, in order for Scriptures to be applied correctly, the Scriptures must be rightly dissected and interpreted.

Many times believers do very stupid things when attempting to demonstrate their spiritual power. They see something God did for someone else, or they take something God said out of context and try to apply it to their own situation. They desire to see a sign from God or witness a miracle in their own lives by God. (If you are saved and have been delivered from sin, you have already witnessed a miracle.)

God has already proven Himself. His record of accomplishment is recorded in the pages of the Bible. Only wicked and adulterous people seek after miracles. That is not to say that God does not do miracles today, but He never told us to seek after them. He did tell us to seek the Kingdom of God and its righteousness and seek those things that are above and not those things on earth. It's that priority thing once again.

John 20:29 *Jesus saith unto him, Thomas, because thou hast seen me, thou hast believed: blessed are they that have not seen, and yet have believed.*

John 20:30 *And many other signs truly did Jesus in the presence of his disciples, which are not written in this book:*

John 20:31 *But these are written, that ye might believe that Jesus is the Christ, the Son of God; and that believing ye might have life through his name.*

Exam Part 4: Test of Worship Exclusivity
Objective: To test your faithfulness and commitment to serving God only. To demonstrate that you will not sell out to the devil for power, position, and possessions.

Well, the devil then thought, *This dude has got it going on! I can use him in my kingdom.*

Then the devil tried to tempt Jesus, *"I have an extraordinary opportunity for you. I can make you richer and more powerful than Solomon was."*

Jesus simply replied, *"Dude, you must not know who I am. You better ask somebody."*

Mathew 4:8 *Again, the devil taketh him up into an exceeding high mountain, and showed him all the kingdoms of the world, and the glory of them;*

Mathew 4:9 *And saith unto him, All these things will I give thee, if thou wilt fall down and worship me.*

In this final part of the exam, Jesus was challenged to see if he would sell out to serve the god of this world for worldly success. When the devil offered the kingdoms of the world to Jesus in exchange for his allegiance and servitude, Jesus understood that the kingdoms of the world were already his to have. Jesus understood that the devil was only in temporary possession and control of the world. Jesus reasoned clearly and thus thought, *"Why should I bow down to Satan to get something that is already mine?* And with that thought in mind,

Mathew 4:10 *Jesus said unto him, Get thee hence, Satan: for it is written, Thou shalt worship the Lord thy God, and him only shalt thou serve.*

Jesus then told the devil, *"I will only serve God and only do His Will. There is nothing you can offer me to make me do otherwise."*

The devil saw that Jesus had scored 100% on every part of the exam. He exclaimed, *"This dude is nothing but the Truth"*. He then departed in disgust, realizing that his own days as ruler of this world were numbered and it was only a matter of time before he would be dethroned and cast into everlasting torment. He hastily departed from Jesus and went about his business of deceiving the world and others in it.

The devil has since gone out and deceived many successful people in this world (celebrities in particular). They have accepted Satan's proposition. They have sold their soul for material success. They have bowed down to the devil and allowed him to use their mind, body, talents, and resources to fill the world with images and ideas that reflect only the character of the devil. They serve as idol gods, role models, and evangelists to promote the gospel of Satan not God's Word.

The key thing to observe about how Jesus aced his exam is that Jesus truly knew the Word of God and understood how to rightly apply it to each situation. That is why he repeatedly said, "It is written" and then quoted the appropriate Scripture, to squash the lie Satan was trying to use to trick him. Eve on the other hand, was ignorant of what God actually said, and Adam was mentally out to lunch because he was so mesmerized by his super sexy sex-toy called Eve.

CHAPTER NINE
The Curse of Evil

The Crime Scene Investigation (CSI Eden)

Adam was the first person God interrogated when He began to investigate the crime scene in the Garden of Eden. Adam was the person God had assigned to keep His garden in check. Adam was the security guard of the garden. God was interested in identifying the security leak. Adam pointed the finger at Eve and threw her right under the bus, head first. Adam tried to make her responsible for his wrongdoing and thus cover up the fact that he was sleeping on the job and did not live up to his responsibility.

Next God interrogated Eve. Eve in turn, pointed the finger at the serpent. God did not bother to ask the devil why he did what he did because he understood that the devil was just doing his job. Satan roams about the earth seeking anyone he can deceive and devour.

Therefore, God decided to cut through the chase and started cursing everyone who was involved in the crime. That does not mean that God went off in a rage using profanity and dropping "F" bombs all over the place. A curse is something that inflicts harm, punishment, evil, or bad will on someone. A curse can be forever, or it can be temporary. There can be a remedy to a curse too, and that remedy can be either a temporary or a permanent solution.

The curse that God put on Adam and Eve from the natural side was a curse that would be experienced by humans throughout all generations. However, the spiritual side of that curse was curable. Although that cure was not readily available to Adam, God had already made plans to deliver the solution to humanity for reversing the curse and curing us of our sinful nature. That cure was the blood of Jesus.

Curse of The Devil

The last person He addressed was the first one God had cursed, and that was the devil.

Genesis 3:14 And the LORD God said unto the serpent, Because thou hast done this, thou art cursed above all cattle, and above every beast of the field; upon thy belly shalt thou go, and dust shalt thou eat all the days of thy life:

God prophetically cursed the devil indicating that Satan would forever be a dirty lowdown scumbag.

Then God told him He would cause him and the woman to be enemies and at odds with one another. In the verse below, God was not referring to Eve as being the woman. The key to understanding this part of the curse rests in the latter part of the verse that, declares that the offspring of the woman would crush Satan's head.

Genesis 3:15-16 And I will put enmity (dislike, opposition) between you and the woman and between your offspring and hers; he will crush your head, and you will strike at his heel.

Who Is the Offspring?

This offspring is not talking about Eve's children. None of her children ever crushed Satan's head. Crushing Satan's head implies, spiritually and legally defeating the devil. The only offspring of a woman that ever defeated Satan in this way, was Jesus. Therefore, Jesus was the offspring that the Scripture is referring to here.

Now if Jesus was the offspring, then was Mary the woman? No! Because it also said, that God would make the woman and Satan enemies. Satan and Mary were never at odds with each other. Satan never launched an attack on Mary. When Jesus was a toddler, Satan by using King Herod tried to kill Jesus, but he never went after Mary. Therefore, Mary is not the woman this verse is referring to.

I have thus ruled out ~~Eve~~ and ~~Mary~~ as being the woman, which leaves only one other qualified candidate. To understand who this candidate is, you must first understand that this is a prophetic utterance. That means that it is a prophecy. God is foretelling that Jesus will defeat Satan. With that in mind, the only other woman that this verse could be talking about is the nation Israel.

Who Is The Woman?

In the *Book of Revelation, Chapter 12*, the nation of Israel is depicted as *"a woman clothed with the **sun**, and the **moon** under her feet, and upon her head a crown of **twelve** stars"*.

*Revelation 12:1 And there appeared a great wonder in heaven; a woman clothed with the **sun**, and the **moon** under her feet, and upon her head a crown of **twelve stars**:*

I will decode this symbolism a little later, but for now, I want you to understand that the verse is speaking on a prophetic level. It is referring to a symbolic woman. The nation of Israel is the nation that symbolically gave birth to Jesus the Messiah, who came forth from the spiritual womb of the tribe of Judah. Therefore, Jesus is spiritually, symbolically, and ancestrally depicted as the offspring of the woman, Israel.

*Genesis 37:9 And he dreamed yet another dream, and told it his brethren, and said, Behold, I have dreamed a dream more; and, behold, the **sun** and the **moon** and the **eleven stars** made obeisance to me.*

*Genesis 37:10 And he told [it] to his father, and to his brethren: and his father rebuked him, and said unto him, What [is] this dream that thou hast dreamed? Shall I and **thy mother** and **thy brethren** indeed come to bow down ourselves to thee to the earth?*

Notice here, that Joseph's father Jacob also known as Israel, immediately understood the symbolism of the dream. He did not ask Joseph to decode or to break the dream down into plain language. He understood clearly that the **sun** was referring to **himself**, the **moon** was referring to **his wife**, who was Joseph's **mother**, and the **eleven stars** referred to the **eleven sons of Israel**, excluding Joseph (which were his brothers).

Therefore, when the same celestial elements are used prophetically in *Revelation 12* concerning the woman clothed with the sun, it ties right back to the prophetic language used in Joseph's dream: The **sun**, the **moon**, and the twelve **stars**. The only difference is that in *Revelation 12*, there are twelve stars instead of eleven, because in *Revelation*, Joseph is included. The man-child that the woman bought forth obviously symbolizes the Messiah, the Christ child.

The Offspring of Christ Is the Church

Galatians 3:16 Now to Abraham and his seed were the promises made. He saith not, And to seeds, as of many; but as of one, <u>And to thy seed, which is Christ</u>.

Galatians 3:29 And <u>if ye [be] Christ's, then are ye Abraham's seed</u>, and heirs according to the promise.

The seed of the woman (Christ) will crush or defeat Satan spiritually, but the devil will attack the followers of Christ. This is what was meant by the devil bruising Christ's heel. It means that the devil will persecute and viciously attack Christ's followers, and some of Christ's followers will experience martyrdom.

Jesus Crushed the Head of Satan

In the fullness of time, Jesus was born as a descendent of Israel, and he destroyed the works and power of the devil from a spiritual perspective. Yet, we see the evil works of the devil still at work on earth. The reason why is that Satan has been defeated in Heaven, but it is the job of believers **(the Church)** to defeat the devil here on earth.

1John 3:8 He that committeth sin is of the devil; for the devil sinneth from the beginning. For this purpose the Son of God was manifested, that he might destroy the works of the devil.

Colossians 2:15 (TLB) In this way God took away Satan's power to accuse you of sin, and God openly displayed to the whole world Christ's triumph at the cross where your sins were all taken away.

Romans 16:20 And the God of peace shall bruise Satan under your feet shortly. The grace of our Lord Jesus Christ be with you. Amen.

The Devil: All Grown Up

Throughout the *Book of Revelation*, John kept seeing various great wonders in Heaven. These were heavenly scenes rather than events that were taking place on earth. What John saw in Heaven, was not necessarily in sync with what was happening on earth at the time. A wonder is *something wonderful or wondrous that makes you wonder,* **"What in heaven is that?"** Therefore, when John saw one of these heavenly visions, he would say to himself, *"I wonder what that is?"*

Revelation 12:3 *And there appeared another wonder in heaven; and behold a great red dragon, having seven heads and ten horns, and seven crowns upon his heads.* (And when John saw that, he said, "I wonder what in Heaven is that?")

Revelation 12:4 And his tail drew the third part of the stars of heaven, and did cast them to the earth: and the dragon stood before the woman which was ready to be delivered, for to devour her child as soon as it was born.

Notice that in the beginning in the Garden of Eden, Satan was a sly and cunning **serpent**. In *Revelation 12:3*, he has grown into **a mon-**

strous beast. He has become **a great red dragon** wielding great power and authority. At this stage, he has an entourage of movers and shakers who have pledged allegiance to his diabolical alliances and schemes.

Satan's goal is still the same as it has always been. He wants to be the sole ruler of this world. In order for him to succeed in his mission, he has to either gain control over the designated ruler, which is now the Church, or he has to subdue or eliminate the Church.

Apostolic vs. the Apostate Church

The Church that Jesus established and commissioned to represent Him on earth is the **Apostolic Church**. This is the group of true believers in Christ that subscribe to and adhere to the Doctrine and teachings of Christ and the Apostles of Christ. This church is obscure and difficult to identify as a whole. Many claim to be part of this church, but their lifestyles and lack of fruitfulness suggest otherwise.

The **Apostate Church** is the **counterfeit** church. They call themselves the church and falsely represent themselves as the genuine Church of Christ, but they follow teachings that are contrary to those prescribed by Christ.

In the Apostate Church, you can have your cake and eat it also while smoking your cigar and drinking your beer at the altar. You can be a member of this church and still live your life however you please. True repentance is not required. You can simply do penance instead. You just have to say that you believe in Christ, but it is not necessary to really do the things he commands because they will say, "God knows their heart and no one is perfect".

This church can also be difficult to identify. On the surface, it looks like it is authentic. However, when you closely examine its doctrine and the lifestyles those in it live, you will begin to realize that something is fundamentally wrong with that picture. When you compare it to the Biblical church and compare its doctrine to Biblical doctrine, that is when you discover what is wrong with the picture. It is a counterfeit.

This disingenuous church body is **antichrist**. Antichrist means that it is against or opposed to Christ and is offered as a **substitute** or **alternative** to Christ. It is thus counterfeit. It presents itself as genuine, but it is fundamentally flawed in doctrine, practices, and devoid of the Spirit of God.

Satan was Kicked Out of Heaven

Revelation 12:7 And there was war in heaven: Michael and his angels fought against the dragon; and the dragon fought and his angels,

Revelation 12:8 And prevailed not; neither was their place found any more in heaven.

Revelation 12:9 And the great dragon was cast out, that old serpent, called the devil, and Satan, which deceiveth the whole world: he was cast out into the earth, and his angels were cast out with him.

Therefore, we can see that Heaven has handled its business of defeating the devil in the spiritual realm and we can see that Satan was also cast down to earth into the domain of man. We are responsible for what is permitted or not permitted on earth. We still see the works of the devil being manifested on earth because we have been collaborating with the devil by allowing him to use our minds and bodies to continuously spread evil. Instead of us destroying the works of evil, we are allowing the works of evil to destroy us. Instead of defeating the devil, we are working in partnership with him by allowing him to use us.

The power of the devil rests in sin, death, the grave, Hell, lies, and deception. Jesus defeated sin by living a totally sinless life. He defeated death, the grave, and Hell by resurrecting from the dead and then ascending back to Heaven. He defeated lies and deception by exposing them with the Word of Truth. He thereby crushed the head of the devil.

Jesus has successfully crushed Satan's head, but what is left to be destroyed is the devil's tail, which consists of his demonic forces and the people who continue to follow him. The saints of God failing to effectively use the power of the Holy Spirit and the Word of God against Satan's army is what is empowering Satan's kingdom to continue thriving.

If the Church as a whole was doing what Jesus and Paul did, the devil would be out of gas by now. If one believer has the power to put a thousand demons to flight and two believers can put ten thousand to flight, imagine how much damage just ten percent of the Body of Christ could do to put the kingdom of darkness out of business! If the collective power that is lying dormant in believers were converted to electrical energy, we would have enough power to light up the world. Maybe, that is why Jesus said that we are indeed the light of the world.

A Child Is Born That Will Rule the World

In the fullness of time, when the world stage was set to present the star of the show, Mary, the biological mother of the Messiah and the nation Israel, his symbolic mother, delivered a male child named Jesus.

Revelation 12:2 And she being with child cried, travailing in birth, and pained to be delivered.

Revelation 12:5 And she brought forth a man child, who was to rule all nations with a rod of iron: and her child was caught up unto God, and to his throne.

What these two verses are communicating is that the time had come for the Messiah to be born into the world. **The woman (Israel)** symbolically gave birth to Jesus, and after Jesus completed his mission, he ascended into the clouds and was caught up to Heaven to sit on the throne of God.

Revelation 12:13 And when the dragon saw that he was cast unto the earth, he persecuted the woman which brought forth the man child.

Revelation 12:14 And to the woman were given two wings of a great eagle, that she might fly into the wilderness, into her place, where she is nourished for a time, and times, and half a time, from the face of the serpent.

After Jesus returned to Heaven, at the appointed time, He sent the Holy Ghost as he had promised, to dwell in the hearts of all those who believe in him and obey him. This gift of the Holy Ghost ushered in **the Church age**. Then **the natural Israel** (the descendants of Jacob that believe in Christ) and **the spiritual Israel** (the Gentile believers) became **the Apostolic Church, the new spiritual Israel** and **the symbolic woman.**

1 Corinthians 12:13 For by one Spirit are we all baptized into one body, whether we be Jews or Gentiles, whether we be bond or free; and have been all made to drink into one Spirit.

Eventually, **the woman** who is now depicted as **the Church** (**the spiritual Israel**) was persecuted by the world system, the Roman Empire. The church was then scattered all over the world (the wilderness).

Revelation 12:6 And the woman fled into the wilderness, where she hath a place prepared of God, that they should feed her there a thousand two hundred and threescore days.

Ezekiel 6:8 "*But I will let a few of my people escape destruction, and they will be scattered among the nations of the world.*

Ezekiel 6:9 Then when they are exiled among the nations, they will remember me. They will recognize how hurt I am by their unfaithful hearts and lustful eyes that long for their idols. Then at last they will hate themselves for all their detestable sins.

Ezekiel 6:10 They will know that I alone am the LORD and that I was serious when I said I would bring this calamity on them.

God knew in advance that His Church was going to be persecuted by Satan. So long before it ever happened, He made prearrangements and reservations in the wilderness (meaning they were scattered among the nations) for a remnant of the Church to have a safe place of refuge. He declared this refuge well in advance through the mouth of Ezekiel.

Who Are the Offspring of the Devil? (1John 3:7-10) & (John 8:41-44)

Those that commit sin is of the devil because whosoever is born of God doth not commit sin. Whosoever do not do righteousness is not of God. Those that do the deeds of their father the devil are the children of the devil.

To clarify, if you habitually practice doing sinful things, then that qualifies you as a genuine sinner. However, if you are a born again believer in Christ, and if you incidentally commit a sinful act and asks God for forgiveness, God sees you as a believer and not a sinner. He sees you as a believer because you are striving to live right, although you still from time to time struggle with sin and are overcome by certain sinful acts. Nevertheless, if as a believer, you return to habitually and willfully sinning, then you are willfully disobeying God.

Although, you are under God's grace, the practice of willful sinning and disobedience can bring harmful evil effects into your life that will eventually cause you to get so far off into left field where you then reach a point of no return. That is what happened to the devil and to the children of Israel. It is a dangerous thing to abuse God's grace.

1John 3:7 Little children, let no man deceive you: he that doeth righteousness is righteous, even as he is righteous.

1John 3:8 He that committeth sin is of the devil; for the devil sinneth from the beginning. For this purpose the Son of God was manifested, that he might destroy the works of the devil.

1 John 3:9 Whosoever is born of God doth not commit sin; for his seed remaineth in him: and he cannot sin, because he is born of God.

1 John 3:10 In this the children of God are manifest, and the children of the devil: whosoever doeth not righteousness is not of God, neither he that loveth not his brother.

The Curse of the Woman

The curse of Eve and Adam had both natural and spiritual implications. God did not just curse Adam and Eve alone. He cursed all men and women for all generations. Adam represented the entire human race. Every other human came from his lineage. So technically and biologically, we all link back to Adam and Eve, which mean that we all are genetically related. We all came from the same source.

Therefore, spiritually and genetically, the sinful nature of Adam and Eve was hereditarily passed on to all generations, and their curse became a multi-generational curse. That is why all women experience labor pains associated with childbirth, and why we have to work for a living.

Romans 5:12 (NLT) When Adam sinned, sin entered the world. Adam's sin brought death, so death spread to everyone, for everyone sinned.

Romans 3:23 For all have sinned, and come short of the glory of God;

Genesis 3:16 Unto the woman he said, I will greatly multiply thy sorrow and thy conception; in sorrow thou shalt bring forth children; and thy desire shall be to thy husband, and he shall rule over thee.

The natural side of this curse determined that giving birth to a child would be a very painful experience. A woman would also desire to control her husband, but he would be in control over her. In the spiritual sense, the spiritual woman Israel also had to experience pain and suffering in bringing forth spiritual children.

In the *Fourth chapter of Genesis*, a similar thing was said to Cain. However, this time it was related to sin desiring to control Cain. God told Cain that he must control sin and be the master of it. This is true of all of us. *Sin desires to control us, but instead, we must exercise control over it.* The very same thing was true of Adam and Eve. Sin was lying in wait at the door of their minds, waiting for a prime opportunity to enter. When we become curious, angry, tempted, or enticed by or about something that is wrong, sin is waiting at the door to influence and take control of our thoughts. If we let these evil thoughts enter our mind and obey what they suggest, it will cause us to bring forth sin.

Sin puts enmity between God and us. However, if we do not entertain evil thoughts to begin with, then such thoughts will not enter our mind at all. Nevertheless, often we are bombarded with evil thoughts and imaginations, and we do not always know where these thoughts originate. When we become aware of its presence, however, we are instructed by the Word of God *to cast down imaginations, and every high thing that exalts itself against the knowledge of God, and bringing into captivity every thought to the obedience of Christ; (2Corinthians 10:5)*

Genesis 4:7 If thou doest well, shalt thou not be accepted? and if thou doest not well, sin lieth at the door. And unto thee shall be his desire, and thou shalt rule over him.

Genesis 4:7 (NLT) "You will be accepted if you do what is right. But if you refuse to do what is right, then watch out! Sin is crouching at the door, eager to control you. But you must subdue it and be its master."

The Curse of Man

Genesis 3:17 And unto Adam he said, Because thou hast hearkened unto the voice of thy wife, and hast eaten of the tree, of which I commanded thee, saying, Thou shalt not eat of it: cursed is the ground for thy sake; in sorrow shalt thou eat of it all the days of thy life;

Genesis 3:18 Thorns also and thistles shall it bring forth to thee; and thou shalt eat the herb of the field;

Genesis 3:19 In the sweat of thy face shalt thou eat bread, till thou return unto the ground; for out of it wast thou taken: for dust thou art, and unto dust shalt thou return.

God starts out by telling Adam why He was cursing him. It was because he listened to some contrary foolishness that his wife presented to him, and Adam did what she suggested. This was Eve's way of exercising her desire to control her husband through the use of her power to influence him.

Adam was supposed to exercise his authority over Eve and put her in check. He was supposed to say to Eve, *"Didn't God tell us not to mess with that tree? Why have you disobeyed God? What part of that did you not understand"?* If Adam had done the responsible thing, he would have prevented sin and evil from ever entering the earth. Going back to my analogy of Adam being the sheriff, if Adam had arrested or rebuked Eve, he would have prevented sin and evil from going any farther.

Adam had the primary responsibility of maintaining law and order, and as long as he was doing his job faithfully, God would have been faithful to provide a remedy and solution for whatever situation Adam had to deal with, including his wife's sin against God. It is evident that God would have provided a solution to demonstrate His love, forgiveness, and grace. This is evident because that is exactly what God did with both Adam and Eve who sinned against Him. He did not physically kill them, He punished them instead. When our children do wrong, we don't kill them for doing wrong (although sometimes we want to), instead we punish them to teach them a lesson and correct the error of their ways.

Nevertheless, they did immediately die spiritually. They were separated from the Presence of God and separated from the spiritual food source of life, which was the Tree of Life. Death is separation from the life source, so God was saying to Adam, *"The reason I am punishing you is because you listened to your wife rather than doing what I, your God, commanded you not to do, and that is why you are being cursed"*. God told Adam, *"Dude, you are supposed to listen to and obey God only. What was so difficult about that?*

Adam was distracted by Eve's breathtaking beauty. When a man is distracted, he loses focus of what is most important and what is priority. The most important thing Adam should have focused on was keeping God's commandment and maintaining a harmonious relationship with God. Women and money are two of the most powerful things that cause men to become distracted from focusing on the biggest priority in life, which is God, and fulfilling His will and purpose for their life.

God was not so concerned with what Eve did but he was focused on what Adam did not do. Adam did not fulfill his obligation and responsibility to God. God holds the man primarily responsible for keeping the earth in order and in alignment with the will of God. Likewise, God is not so concerned about, what the unsaved world is doing. He is most concerned about what His church of believers are doing and not doing. Sinners are doing what you expect sinners to do; (They sin! That is what they do). The saints are failing miserably at what God expects the saints to be doing and not doing. God expects the saints to live holy, stop sinning, and preach the gospel to sinners.

Going back to the text again *Genesis 3:17 ...cursed is the ground for thy sake; in sorrow shalt thou eat of it all the days of thy life;*

Genesis 3:18 Thorns also and thistles shall it bring forth to thee; and thou shalt eat the herb of the field;

Genesis 3:19 In the sweat of thy face shalt thou eat bread, till thou return unto the ground; for out of it wast thou taken: for dust thou art, and unto dust shalt thou return.

On the natural side of this curse, God was saying to Adam and to all humanity that Adam's food source would come from the ground, but that ground will be cursed. The ground would produce thorns and thistles, causing man to work hard to produce food to eat.

(This is why I am so happy we have progressed from the agricultural and industrial age, into the information age. In the information age, there are many opportunities to make a living from the comfort of your air-conditioned home and thus avoid all that hard work and sweating. Thank God that He gave man a mind that can devise witty and ingenious inventions that takes the edge off this curse. We still may have to work, but now some of us can work smart rather than hard. (But there are still millions who still have to do hard labor.)

However, on the spiritual side of this curse, the thorns and thistles have spiritual meanings.

Mathew 13:18 Hear ye therefore the parable of the sower.

Mathew 13:19 When any one heareth the word of the kingdom, and understandeth it not, then cometh the wicked one, and catcheth away that which was sown in his heart. This is he which received seed by the way side.

Mathew 13:22 He also that received seed among the thorns is he that heareth the word; and the care of this world, and the deceitfulness of riches, choke the word, and he becometh unfruitful.

This parable identifies **the ground** as the **heart of a man**. The **thorns and thistles** represent man's desire for **worldly pursuits, material things**, and **evil and lustful desires**. They represent the **temptations of the world**.

Therefore, we are told we have to work hard to bring forth righteousness in our lives because our hearts are full of evil thoughts and desires, so we must struggle daily in a battle to overcome the sinful evil desires that lurk deeply within us. We having to struggle with evil forces in our effort to produce good fruits of righteousness is the result of the disobedience of Adam and Eve.

Mark 7:20 *And he said, That which cometh out of the man, that defileth the man.*

Mark 7:21 *For from within, out of the heart of men, proceed evil thoughts, adulteries, fornications, murders,*

Mark 7:22 *Thefts, covetousness, wickedness, deceit, lasciviousness, an evil eye, blasphemy, pride, foolishness:*

Mark 7:23 *All these evil things come from within, and defile the man.*

1 John 2:15 *Love not the world, neither the things that are in the world. If any man love the world, the love of the Father is not in him.*

1 John 2:16 *For all that is in the world, the lust of the flesh, and the lust of the eyes, and the pride of life, is not of the Father, but is of the world.*

1 John 2:17 *And the world passeth away, and the lust thereof: but he that doeth the will of God abideth for ever.*

1 Timothy 6:9 *But they that will be rich fall into temptation and a snare, and into many foolish and hurtful lusts, which drown men in destruction and perdition.*

1 Timothy 6:10 *For the love of money is the root of all evil: which while some coveted after, they have erred from the faith, and pierced themselves through with many sorrows.*

CHAPTER TEN
Living Holy Before God and Restoring the Garden

We must cultivate the ground of our hearts by plucking out the weeds (which are our evil thoughts and desires) from our heart and planting instead the righteous seeds (the Word of Truth) therein. By consistently uprooting weeds, planting good seeds, and then fertilizing, and watering them, we will then consistently produce perpetual crops of righteousness in our lives.

Our heart is our spiritual Garden of Eden. In the midst of that garden is the Tree of Life, which is the Word of God. Also in the midst of that garden is the Tree of Knowledge of Good and Evil. This tree invites us to rely on our human intellect, worldly ideas, human ideologies, and philosophies to determine what we should consider to be good and evil. The Tree of Life represents our trusting in the Word of God to determine what is good and what is evil. Everything we are commanded or advised to do through the Word of God is good. Conversely, everything the Scriptures commands or instructs us not to do is evil. Can it get any simpler than that?

Jesus totally relied on and trusted what the Word of God said. That is why He constantly said, *"It, is, written.* Jesus clearly showed us how to overcome evil. We will be delivered from all evil if we have our hearts filled with the Word of God, follow Jesus' example, and consistently obey God's Word.

Give Us This Day Our Daily Bread

Our daily bread is twofold. It relates to both our physical and spiritual nourishment. We are commanded not to worry about tomorrow and only be concerned about what we need today. Tomorrow will never come, yesterday is gone, but today is here right now. Stop looking for tomorrow because we will never see tomorrow. Every time tomorrow is scheduled to arrive, today keeps showing up in its place. (Have you noticed that unique phenomenon yet?)

Every night I go to bed hoping to see tomorrow, but when I wake up the next day, I notice that no one is calling it 'tomorrow'. What was supposed to be 'tomorrow' everyone is calling it 'today'. The next time someone says they are going to do something for you tomorrow, ask them, do they mind doing it today because tomorrow never seems to arrive. Therefore, forget about tomorrow because it does not exist. Tomorrow is only a temporary reference to another 'today' that will soon arrive.

God knows exactly what we need today, and He has promised to give us what we need for today. God knows that we have physical needs and need physical food for our bodies. Yet, the real bread we need is not sliced bread, or (money) bread, but the bread of life, which is the Word of God. This is why Jesus said that man does not live by bread alone (food), but by every word that proceeds from the mouth of God.

The Word of God is our spiritual food, and it causes us to live forever. Spiritual food for our soul is far more important than the food we eat to keep our bodies alive just for today. If you only feed your body and starve your soul to death, you will die three times. You will experience first a spiritual death, then a physical death, and finally, eternal death. On the other hand, if your soul is well nourished by the Word of God, you will die only once, and afterwards, you'll live forever with God.

Therefore, we are commanded to not worry about tomorrow and to not worry about our basic needs. Our Heavenly Father is well aware of what we need. Even our earthly parents are fully aware that we need food, clothing, and shelter. When a child comes into this world, they are not worried about these basic needs. They trust that their parents are going to provide these things without them having to constantly worry about them.

The child has the responsibility of learning the various skills and knowledge needed to become a productive, independent, and mature individual. So likewise, God promises that if we focus primarily on learning the principles of His kingdom, learning to live righteously, and learning to love one another, He will automatically provide us with our daily necessities. He also promises that if we ask Him for anything that is according to His will, He will gladly give us that.

However, God is primarily and most concerned about us spiritually growing, developing, and learning how to responsibly use the things he entrusts to us. When you give a child something that he is not mature enough to understand the proper and intended use of, he will inevitably abuse it, misuse it, and possible injure himself and others.

God does not give us everything we ask for because if the truth were told, many of us are not quite ready to receive certain things. If you give a fool or a financially illiterate person a huge amount of money, he will blow it all on foolish things and soon return to being broke. This is precisely why so many people that win the lottery soon return to being busted and disgusted.

Overcoming sin and eradicating evil from our lives is not a one-shot deal. Every day offers us a new challenge and also a new opportunity for the devil to tempt and test us. Each day is a new opportunity for us to wake up, serve, and glorify God in all that we think, do, and say. It is also another opportunity for the devil to try to get us to do his will instead. Just because you may have had a successful day today defeating sin and evil in your life, the devil and his cohorts will be right back at you the next day and every chance they get. This is why it is important to pray for what you need for today.

Every Spirit Must Be X-rayed By the Demon Detector
Even when we are fast asleep, we are sometimes bombarded with ungodly and evil dreams and nightmares. I guess that is one of the reasons God said we should always pray. Evil is always lying in wait for an opportunity to enter our minds and hearts and gain entrance into the world through us.

We must learn to clearly identify every spirit that knocks at the door of our minds. Not every spirit is of God or from God. That is why we have to learn to discern spirits by learning how to examine them. We need to install spiritual demon detectors at every access point. The Word of God is the best demon detector. Any spirit that presents information, thoughts, or ideas to your mind that are contrary and inconsistent with the Word of God are neither of God nor from God.

Just because a spirit presents information from the Word of God does not mean that it is of or from God. That is precisely how Satan approached both Eve and Jesus. He misused information from the Word of God to convince them that he was presenting the truth. He remixed the Word of God. He took it either out of context or added words, subtracted words, or inverted, subverted, or perverted the Word of

God. That is what you have to look out for. Satan is a master of lies and deception and a master of word manipulation.

We Must Become Skillful Soldiers

Believers must study the Word of God diligently and learn how to examine, dissect, analyze, and interpret the Word of Truth rightly. The Word of God is the only offensive weapon we have available to us to defeat the devil. All the rest of our spiritual armor is defensive and protective gear, which does include the shield of faith, the helmet of salvation, and the breastplate of righteousness.

Ephesians 6:13 Wherefore take unto you the whole armor of God, that ye may be able to withstand in the evil day, and having done all, to stand.

Ephesians 6:14 Stand therefore, having your loins girt about with truth, and having on the breastplate of righteousness;

Ephesians 6:15 And your feet shod with the preparation of the gospel of peace;

Ephesians 6:16 Above all, taking the shield of faith, wherewith ye shall be able to quench all the fiery darts of the wicked.

Ephesians 6:17 And take the helmet of salvation, and the sword of the Spirit, which is the word of God:

Just as a highly trained soldier must know how to use a sword proficiently and skillfully, we must likewise know, as did Jesus and Paul, how to skillfully use the Word of God. If we fail to develop that skill, the devil will constantly defeat us in every area of our lives where we are ignorant of the truth.

Forgive Us Our Trespasses

As believers in Christ, we must grow from **spiritual infancy** to **spiritual adulthood**. This is a lifelong process. Consequently, we will make mistakes and sin against God, one another, and ourselves during the process. **Forgiveness** is the key that makes these wrongs right. God forgives us contingent upon our forgiving those who sin against us. He said, *if we do not forgive others, then neither does our Heavenly Father forgive us.*

Mathew 6:14 For if ye forgive men their trespasses, your heavenly Father will also forgive you:

Mathew 6:15 But if ye forgive not men their trespasses, neither will your Father forgive your trespasses.

When we refuse to forgive, we harbor evil, and evil is like a spiritual cancer. If we allow it to remain in our heart, it will metastasize and affect other areas of our life. Unforgiveness is like leaven in bread. A little unforgiveness can rise and develop into anger, resentment, malice, hatred, and other evil diseases.

Evil feeds on our carnal and lustful appetites, our uncontrolled emotions, our greed, our ignorance, our lack of knowledge, our anger, and our envy. Evil is always lurking, waiting for one of these entry points to present a negative opportunity. Keeping evil out of our lives requires us to be diligent, vigilant, and ever serious about living holy and obediently, following every commandment, law, principle, and precept of God.

Lead Us Not into Temptation

Satan is the one who tempts us. God tempts no one. We are tempted when we are enticed by our own lustful desires. When we decide to engage or act on those lustful desires, that is when and how we get caught up in sin.

God leads us toward and into righteousness. Nevertheless, He does allow the devil to tempt us as He clearly demonstrated with Job. If we walk in accordance to the Spirit of Love and the Spirit of Truth, we will not yield to our carnal and lustful desires. The only reason sin can overtake us is because we actually want to do the sinful things the devil suggests. We pretend that "the devil made us do it", but the reality is, that is just the excuse we use to pretend that we did not want to do it.

The devil can only tempt you to do that which you already want to do. For example, a person who loves doing cocaine will be tempted by one line of cocaine sitting on a glass table. Yet, a person who does not care for cocaine can be in a warehouse full of cocaine and will not be the least bit tempted to indulge.

God is not stupid, and yes, He knows our heart as well as our weaknesses. We are weak in certain areas of our lives because we do not exercise our spiritual muscles. Yes, we tend to be lazy and trifling when it comes to being spiritually fit and developed. We neglect to study the Word of God attentively and regularly, and then practice doing what that Word of God instructs.

We love to watch the preacher's workout in the pulpit and on TV and cheer him on. It is like going to the gym and watching others work out, but rarely working out ourselves. If we study His Word, learn to interpret it correctly, and obey God's Word, the Word and the Holy Spirit together will lead us away from temptation and effectively deliver us from all evil.

Deliver Us from All Evil

Finally, after all is said and done, we all sincerely want to be delivered from the bad effects of evil. Nevertheless, many of the sinful things we engage in, we actually enjoy. The pleasure that sin offers is what makes us want to indulge in sin, but if we refuse to give into the lustful desire, the evil desire will eventually go away.

However, the Bible tells us in *James 4:7 to resist the devil and he will flee.* When the devil sees that he is not going to score with you, he moves on to a more willing vessel. All we have to do is obey the applicable Word that speaks to the temptation or test we are confronted with. God delivers us from evil by us obeying the Word of Truth and walking in the Spirit of Love. Steadfast obedience to the Word causes us to be devoid and free of all evil, makes us genuinely holy and righteous in the sight of God, and enables us to consistently reflect the image and likeness of God.

Saul, The Original Terrorist of the Early Church

The Apostle Paul (formerly known as Saul) was considered an evil terrorist before his conversion and transformation. Believers feared Saul more than they feared God or the devil. The devil only had the power to deceive and trick the believers into doing stupid stuff. However, Saul was on a relentless mission to stamp out the advancement of the Kingdom of God on earth and its followers. He was on his way to Damascus to obtain the legal authority to arrest Christians and have them jailed and killed. Saul was the poster child of Christian terrorism. He was a Christian's worst nightmare.

Although what Saul was doing was obviously evil, God did not see Saul as an evil man. Saul was doing what he was doing because in his heart he thought it was right. Based on his cultural and religious upbringing, Saul understood Judaism to be the true religion of God. In his mind, anything else was heresy, so he was determined to prevent the spread of it. God, upon seeing the integrity of Saul's heart, overlooked his overt evil actions.

Meanwhile, Christians stood in great fear of Saul and were most likely praying that God would kill this evil man. What they should have been praying was to have God open Saul's eyes that he might see the truth and be delivered from his evil and misguided agenda.

We often see people doing evil things and want God to retire them from the earth. However, what we fail to realize is that like Saul, they are doing the evil they are doing out of ignorance. We should be praying that all humans be delivered from evil. Who knows? God might just harken to our prayers and miraculously and dramatically intervene in their lives and open their blinded eyes.

This is why Jesus said *to pray for our enemies*, and remember that *all of us who are now believers use to be enemies of God.* Nevertheless, *while we were yet enemies of God, Christ still came and died for our sins* in spite of our obstinate rebellion, ignorance, and evil ways. When Jesus was hanging on the cross, He prayed asking, *"Father, forgive them for they don't have a clue as to what they are doing and who they are doing it to." (Luke 23:34)*

The Greatest Love of All

What greater love is there than this? Jesus willingly gave up his own life, to save the life of others that hated him. Love is kind, considerate, and seeks good will for everyone. Love looks past faults to extract what is good and beneficial. Love is the core nature and character of God, and His character is His image. God created us in His image and wants us to be like Him.

The devil came to beat us down with the club of sin and evil and has disfigured and distorted our God image. Yet, God sent his Son Jesus into the world to crush the head of Satan, restore our image, and give us back the power to defeat all our spiritual enemies.

We are commanded to love one another, including our enemies. While we were yet God's enemy, Christ demonstrated the perfect model of love for us to follow. Love conquers all evil just as truth expels lies and deceptions. Love and Truth are the ultimate weapons for destroying sin and evil.

Conclusion: Final Thoughts

Herein, I have presented many Biblical truths and insights to try to help you understand what you must do to be delivered from the power of sin and evil that is working in and through your life. We ultimately have control over the internal invasion and infestation of evil operating in our lives. We have control over and can prevent our minds, bodies, and resources from being used for evil purposes.

What we have limited control over is others who do allow evil to work and be manifested through them. Although Jesus was God in human form and did not allow sin and evil to operate through His mind and body, He did not override the will of others and prevent them from doing evil even to him. Every person must decide for himself to obey God and reject Satan and his evil intentions.

We do have a great deal of control over how external forces of evil will affect us and what effects they will have on us. We can live a holy and righteous lifestyle that can be as a bright light for others, influencing them to live right as well. Nevertheless, that does not happen by our own power. It happens only by the power of the Spirit of the Lord. Amen!

Now that we are armed with the knowledge and power to overcome and crush evil and sin in our lives, what is most important now is to just do it! The blessing and manifestation of good in our lives is in doing what the Word commands, not just reading about it, thinking about it, talking about it, and confessing it. Yes, all these things are important prerequisites, but the blessing and the manifestation come from the actual doing what the Word of God prescribes.

My Prayer of Deliverance
God, deliver us from evil and cleanse us from all unrighteousness. Your desire is to produce a generation of people who will serve you in spirit and in truth and walk uprightly, thereby following all Your statutes. Your desire is for the earth to be as it was in the Garden of Eden before sin entered it. Your desire is for Your Will to be done on earth as it is in Heaven.

Lord, give Your people the right information and the right understanding of that information. Bless them, so they will obey You and resist the devil. Turn their hearts away from worldly lusts and cause them to diligently pursue after righteousness, holiness, the Kingdom of God, and those things, which are above. Lord cause Your Word to permeate our hearts and let Your righteous blood flow through our veins, so that we may become the righteous generation You have long desired.

Heavenly Father, I love You and thank You and Your Son Jesus for choosing me to produce this work unto Your glory. Keep me in all my ways and bless me to be steadfast, immovable, and always abounding in the work of the Lord. Bless this work to be fruitful and bless souls all over the world. Bless their relationships and empower them to focus steadfastly on establishing Your Kingdom on earth and doing

Your will in their life daily.

I pray for all sinners that they will all come to know you as Lord and savior. I pray for those that are weak in the faith that you strengthen them and cause them to turn from their carnal ways and pursue righteousness with all due diligence. Bless those that are strong and know the Word to continually grow and help others to grow and be strong in the faith.

Finally fellow saint, may the God of peace keep you in perfect peace and deliver you from all evil.

In Jesus' name I pray, forever bless God, amen.

Important Take-Aways and Things To Remember

Excerpt From The Book "Deliver Us From Evil" by Deryl S. Lampkin © 2014 by Deryl S. Lampkin All rights reserved.

Fundamental Rules For Overcoming And Defeating The devil

Rule # 1 Proverb 3:5 Trust in the LORD with all your heart; do not depend on your own understanding.

God has all knowledge, wisdom, and understanding, which qualify him to have all the answers and make all the right decisions. Man's intelligence and the devil's intelligence is terribly limited and flawed. This is why we should trust what God says, rather than what we think or feel. #DSLQuote

Rule # 2 Understand that when God establishes a rule or law, it is not up for debate or revision based on cultural norms, practices, or how times have changed. Times may change, but God's immutable laws do not change with the times. #DSLQuote

Rule # 3 Factual information is objective but understanding of the information is subjective. In other words, truth is truth and what you think, feel, or believe, does not change the truth. If you misinterpret or misunderstand the truth, the truth will still be the truth. Your misunderstanding of the truth just means that you don't really have the truth. You just have your own version of something you believe to be truth but it is not. #DSLQuote

Rule # 4 When the devil offers you something that is forbidden by God or opposes God, he will make it appealing to your flesh, to your eyes, and to you ego. He will sell you on the benefits. How it will make you feel, look, be seen by others, make you rich, famous, popular, etc. He will not show you what it is going to do to you in the end. He is not going to show you what you are forfeiting. #DSLQuote

Rule # 5a (For Men) The devil is fully aware of a woman's seductive power over a man. He understands that a woman is easier to deceive than a man because she processes things sensually and emotionally. Therefore, the strategy he deploys is to use his cunningness to deceive the woman and the woman will use her seductive power to influence the man. #DSLQuote

Rule # 5b (For Women) The love of money is the root of all evil. Love not the world, neither the things that are in the world. The desire and lust for worldly goods, material things, and feel goods; will be the very things the devil will use through the vehicle of men (and women, for those women who prefer women) to entice you to disobey God and do sinful and evil things. #DSLQuote

Rule # 6 If we sin, don't cover it, confess it to God. Don't try to hide it from God because you can't, instead expose it, and God will dispose it. When we try to cover our sins or deny that we have sinned, sin will keep us at odds with God. But if we confess our sins, God is faithful and just to forgive us and cleans us from all unrighteousness. #DSLQuote

Many Of Our Problems Are Our Own Creations

Many of our problems and issues are products that we have manufactured ourselves. In other words, we create our own problems. They come about because of things we do or fail to do; things we say or don't say; things we think or don't think about; and things we think we know and things we don't know. #DSLQuote

The Two Greatest Temptations

Two of the greatest temptations that influences humans to do evil is sex and money. In general, men love sex and women love money. Men use money to get sex and women use sex to get money. Men want to get laid and women want to get paid. #DSLQuote

Responsible Living

In the world, there will always be problems until God exterminates the earth and rid it of all things that offend. But until then, we should be diligently doing our part to change the world for the better. After all, we are the ones that are living on earth and have to put up with all the evil we allow to come into our world and remain in it. #DSLQuote

We can blame it all on the devil and others and make it seem as though someone else is the blame. When we think like that, we are not taking personal responsibility. The devil may have in fact suggested a bad idea to us, but it is us who accepted and acted on the bad idea. The devil does not have any power to make you do anything. We make that ultimate decision. #DSLQuote

What Gets Us In Trouble With God
Our general tendency is to lean towards our own misguided intellectual understanding rather than trusting in the Word of God. This is how sin and death entered our world and ever since then, we have been struggling to be delivered from evil, but it continues to plague us. #DSLQuote

Disobeying God causes us to forfeit those things that God has given us and entrusted to us. #DSLQuote

The Purpose of The Devil
God purposely allows the devil to roam the earth so that the devil can prove who is of God and who is not. Satan is the tempter and tester of humanity. God uses him to reveal what we are made of character wise. If we are truly made of God characteristics, it will be evident when we are tested. If we lack godly character, that too will be evident when we are tested. #DSLQuote

The devil, really is not the problem. The problem is whether we have godly character or not. If we have it, we will defeat the devil and be victorious in every area of our life. If we don't have it, we will suffer defeat. #DSLQuote

Who Shall Dwell With God
Many people go to church, quote Scriptures, and talk the talk. Nevertheless, those that do all those things and walk the walk, are they that will overcome the devil and dwell with God forever. #DSLQuote

It is those that live their life in alignment with the Word and Spirit of God and cease to live according to the ways of the world and after the lusts of the flesh, that will prove by their resistance to the devil and their righteous living, that they belong to God. #DSLQuote

How Going Back To The Beginning Enables Us To Free Ourselves From Sin
I have found that by going back to the beginning and reexamining how sin and evil entered the world, we can more clearly see and understand how to be delivered from evil and how to help others to be set free.

We can rise above evil and overcome it, rather than letting it exercise control over us. #DSLQuote

God Has Given Us The Power To Bind And Loose (Restrain and Permit)

God has authorized us to bind and put a halt to things that should not be happening on earth and to release and unleash things that should be happening on earth. The very reason we are seeing sin and evil running rampant on earth is because we are allowing it to do so. We are not using the power that was delivered to us by Jesus to put a stop to it. #DSLQuote

If You Do Not Learn How To Use The Power You Have, You Will Remain Powerless

You can have a very powerful computer loaded with the most powerful software, but if you don't know how to use what you have, you remain powerless to benefit from all the power you have at you disposal. Therefore, if you have the power of God within you and do not know how to use it, you will remain powerless. #DSLQuote

How Sin, Evil, Righteousness, and all Humans and Spirits Enter The Earth

Sin and evil enters the world through people and through people, it continues to grow and flourish. The Kingdom of God and its righteousness also enters the world through people and through people, it grows and flourish throughout the world. #DSLQuote

We want to be delivered from evil but we keep perpetuating it by continuing to think, speak, and do evil. How can we possibly be delivered from evil when we are the very ones that keep delivering more evil into the world? #DSLQuote

There Is Nothing New Under The Sun

What went wrong in the beginning is the same thing that is continuing to go wrong now. From this perspective, there is nothing new under the sun. #DSLQuote

What Is The Good News

The Son of God has arrived with the keys and power to defeat evil and he has made that power accessible to all those that believe in him and follow his instructions and teachings. #DSLQuote

The Kingdom message was that we no longer have to be prisoners of sin and work like slaves to produce evil. We are now free from the power of sin and free to serve God in spirit and in truth. We now have unfettered access to the resources of God. We can now access God directly and ask for whatever we need, to accomplish his will on earth. That is the Good News. #DSLQuote

How To Rid Your Mind Of Darkness, Evil, And Sinfulness

The more of the information of God we introduce to our mind and put into regular practice, the more the darkness, evil, and sinful things in our mind and heart will vanish from our lives. #DSLQuote

What The Tree Of Knowledge of Good And Evil Represents

The Tree of Knowledge of Good and Evil represents humans leaning toward their own misguided intellectual understanding rather than trusting in what the Word of God says. This source of information comes from the devil. He suggests alternative ideas and solutions contrary to the Word of God. #DSLQuote

Proverb 3:5 Trust in the LORD with all your heart; do not depend on your own understanding.

We Have Become Disciples of Men Rather Than Disciples of Christ

Too many pastors have made us to be disciples of religion and disciples of themselves, rather than Disciples of Christ. Saints have been taught the rudiments and rituals of religion, rather than the principles and precepts of the Kingdom of God. #DSLQuote

Our Foremost Responsibility and Obligation On Earth

Fear God, and keep his commandments: for this is the whole duty of man." (Ecclesiastes 12:13)

The Word Is The Primary Source of All Intelligence

The Word is the primary source of all knowledge, information, and intelligence. Everything that exists anywhere and everywhere was created from and by this intelligence source called the Word and called God. #DSLQuote

God Made The Visible World By Using Things In The Invisible World

Before God created the visible physical world, he first created the invisible spiritual world. He created thrones, powers, principalities, dominions, and an innumerable host of angelic beings. God made the things that are seen in the physical world using invisible things existing in the invisible world. #DSLQuote

God Made Man To Be Like Him And To Establish An Intimate Love Relationship With Him

God had and idea in mind to create and entity that was like him. He wanted this entity to be a physical expression of himself, a hardcopy of the invisible God.

God desired to have a special love relationship with this physical expression of himself. He called this expression, man. #DSLQuote

The Word of God Is The Light That Expels The Dark Evil In Our Heart

The more of the information of God we introduce to our mind and put into regular practice, the more the dark evil and sinful things in our mind and heart will vanish from our lives. #DSLQuote

God Used Himself As The Model For Creating Man

When God created all the other life forms, he simply spoke to the waters and the earth and commanded them to bring forth the appropriate life forms.

But when it came to man, God spoke to himself, and God said, Let us make man in our image, after our likeness: and let them have dominion over the fish of the sea, and over the fowl of the air, and over the cattle, and over all the earth, and over every creeping thing that creepeth upon the earth. Genesis 1:26

Man Is God's Most Prized Creation

From God's point of view, man was the most prized creation of all God's creation. Man was the only creation of God's, given such high and extraordinary honor and glory; not even the angels had such status and even they were created in part to serve man. #DSLQuote

There is no other creature that God refers to as sons of God. There is no other creature he sent his son to die for other than man. The angels are only servants of God.

Redeemed humans are designated to be joint heirs with Christ and to be rulers in the Kingdom of God on earth. These special designations are only granted to redeemed humans.

God Is The Only Entity That Is Qualified To Be Both Father And Son

God the Father fulfills the role of creator and sustainer of the universe and God the Son is the savior of the world. God the Father is the Source and God the Son is the way to connect to the Source. God is the only being in existence that is qualified to fulfill both roles. #DSLQuote

The Holy Spirit Is The Spirit Of Love And Truth United As One

The Holy Spirit is the complete spirit of God. God is a spirit and God is the spirit of love. Jesus is the spirit of truth. These two spirits are one spirit, which is the Holy or complete Spirit of God. Therefore, the Father and the Son equals the Holy Spirit. #DSLQuote

They began as one, they became two separate entities with different roles, purposes, and identity, and then when the mission of the Son was accomplished, they became one Spirit again (The Holy Spirit). #DSLQuote

The Spirit of God is both the form of existence of God and the power of God. #DSLQuote

Consistently Obeying The Word And Spirit of Truth, Transforms Us Into The Image Of God

When we obey the words of truth that the spirit of truth communicates to our spirit, it will produce the fruits of love in our heart. That which is produced in our heart will flow out of our being in the form of words and deeds of life and demonstrations of acts of love. #DSLQuote

When we walk in love, we walk in the spirit. When we walk in the spirit, we walk in unity and harmony with God. When we walk in unity and harmony with God, we become one with God and reflect the image of God. #DSLQuote

Man can only consistently reflect the image of God by consistently obeying what God commands. The more we learn of God's ways and practice them daily, we will become more and more like God. The superimposed image of the devil will begin to dissolve and fade away, the clear image of God will re-emerge in its glory, and we will again look and be like God. #DSLQuote

Jesus Was The Perfect Model Of What A Man Was Created To Be

The Son, which was the Word (the Spirit of Truth) temporarily took on a human form to enable humans to see what God looks like and how he behaves in a human format. This format served as a visual example and model of what God intended for humans to be like. #DSLQuote

Adam Was Created With Male And Female Attributes To Rule And To Submit

When God originally created Adam, he was both male and female. The masculine part of man dominates and rules but the feminine part of man submits, obeys, and assists. This is why when God made the woman, he put the man as head over her and commanded that the wives are to submit to their own husband. #DSLQuote

Man was created to rule over the earth and his household. He can only do that effectively by submitting to God through Christ. #DSLQuote

God Wants Quality People Not Quantity

God is not just interested in large numbers of people, but he is most interested in the earth being populated with righteous living people. God would rather have a few righteous people on earth, rather than to have a great multitude of wicked, rebellious, evildoers. #DSLQuote

God Saves A Multitude, But Only A Remnant Remains Faithful To Him

God will save a large group of people from destruction, however, if some of those in that select group believe not, do not wholly follow God, do not obey the voice of the Lord, or do not please God, they shall be eliminated from the saved group and destroyed. Therefore, salvation without transformation, leads to condemnation and the judgment, and destruction of body, soul, and spirit. #DSLQuote

The Value and Power of Women

Women, in spite of whatever flaws, weaknesses, or issues they may have, they certainly bring unprecedented value to the table of life and the power they possess is nothing to be taken lightly or for granted. #DSLQuote

If you just want to sit, share and debate ideas and information, get a group of men together. But if you really want to get the ball moving and get the job done, get a group of women together. #DSLQuote

Men should love their woman and treat her like a queen, but guard their affections and think with their upper head. #DSLQuote

A man's kryptonite is a woman. A woman is capable of destroying the most powerful of men. Men like Sampson who could defeat a thousand men with the jawbone of an ass, was stripped of his mighty power by one single woman. #DSLQuote

The devil is fully aware of her seductive power over a man. He understood that a woman is easier to deceive than a man. Therefore, his strategy was to use his cunningness to deceive the woman and the woman will use her seductive power to bring down the man. (Awesome strategy) #DSLQuote

About The Author

Deryl S. Lampkin was born and raised in Miami, Florida. He began playing piano at the early age of four. Music has been his foremost passion until he became an avid believer in Christ at age twenty-two. Now God, Christ, and the Word of God is his preeminent interest and first love.

He is multi-talented and is often referred to as "The Hat Man" because he is capable of wearing many different hats. It takes less time for him to tell you what he does not do than it takes to tell you what he does.

During his early years as a believer, his soul thirsted and hungered for truth and revelation. He diligently and tirelessly studied the scriptures 18 to 20 hours a day and God indeed filled him with His Word and Holy Spirit.

At the age of 54, he decided to obtain a bachelor's degree in Internet Marketing from Full Sail University. He was the first and only of his male siblings to obtain a college degree. After fulfilling that goal, he decided to pursue his most passionate goal of becoming an author, spiritual teacher, and thought leader. He currently serves as a Bible study teacher at Kingdom Faith Global Ministries and is scheduled to release his first book entitled "Deliver Us From Evil" November 09, 2014.

He is passionate about helping people to understand the Word of God and teaching them how to effectively apply it to their lives. Many people take to the grave the great treasures that were stored in them. Deryl's ultimate goal is to fulfill the will of God for his life and die empty.

Join My Mailing List

If you have enjoyed this book, leave a positive review on the site where you purchased it, tweet it, like it and share it on Facebook, and encourage the people in your circle to buy it. Last, but not least, live it!

Be sure to visit my website and join my mailing list so that I can keep you updated with new titles as well as, other available events and resources.

Visit www.deryllampkin.com and subscribe to my mailing list.

Thank you for buying and reading this book. May God richly bless your soul and cause you to prosper in all things as you learn to consistently obey his Word.